DINNER IN 5

PETE EVANS

 plum. Pan Macmillan Australia

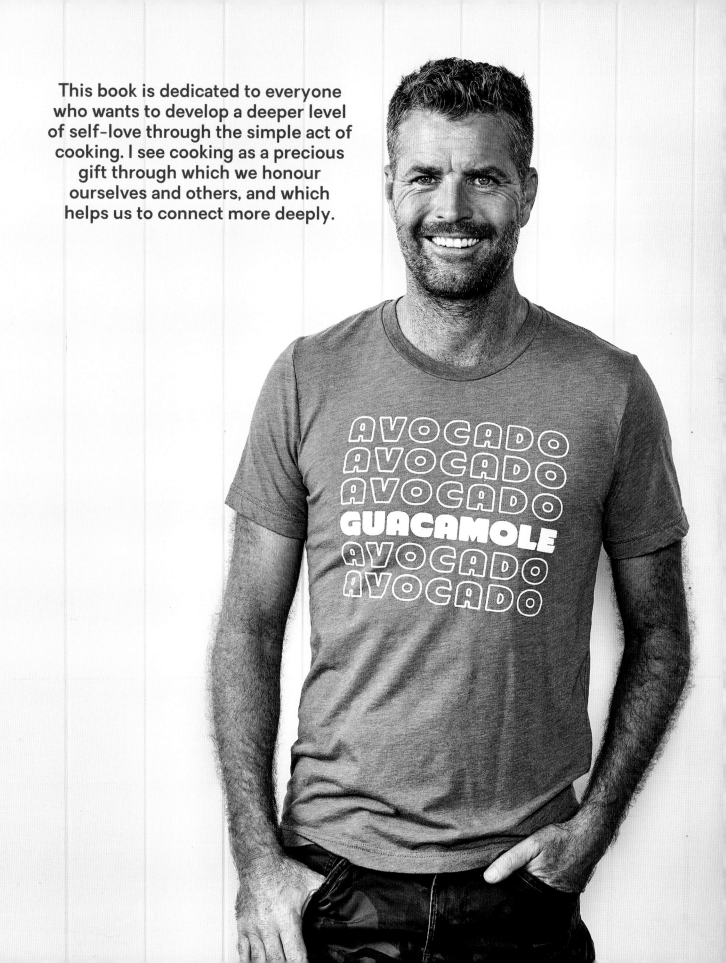

This book is dedicated to everyone who wants to develop a deeper level of self-love through the simple act of cooking. I see cooking as a precious gift through which we honour ourselves and others, and which helps us to connect more deeply.

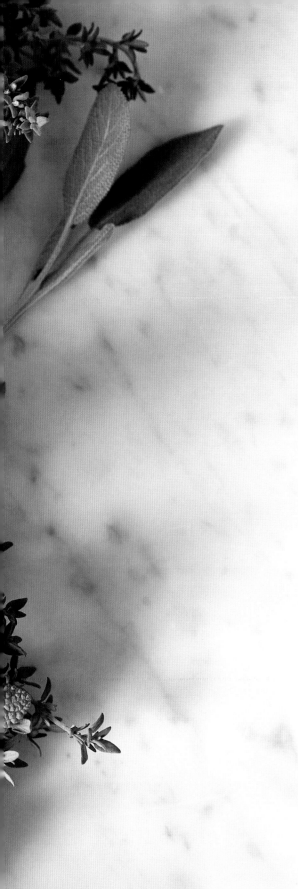

INTRODUCTION

This book is all about simplicity – combining a small number of high-quality, fresh ingredients without sacrificing delicious flavour ...

First of all, I want to thank you for reading this cookbook. By adopting the simple principles outlined here, you and your family are well and truly on the way to sustainable and long-term health.

I am passionate about healthy eating and my main aim is to make it easy and achievable for as wide an array of people as possible. With this book, I want to minimise the fuss and time involved in preparing meals, whether it's for shopping or cooking – after all, time is something we could all use more of. Healthy eating doesn't need to be hard or involve long lists of hard-to-source ingredients. This book is all about simplicity – combining a small number of high-quality, fresh ingredients without sacrificing delicious flavour.

Dinner in 5 makes preparing healthy meals a breeze by stripping each recipe back to five main ingredients. Some feature optional (and equally simple) add-ons, such as a throw-together spice rub or dressing.

What I have learned from the countless meals I have cooked in my lifetime is this: to make food spectacular is pretty simple – and I have done my best to illustrate that with these recipes. You will see there is a section at the back for spice rubs and seasonings. Like the main recipes, each spice rub or seasoning has only a few ingredients. I encourage you to make these ahead of time to keep on standby, as they are the secret to turning a good meal into a great one.

There is also a section featuring delicious sauces, dressings and sides to add to your meals, again to make them a little more special. All the sauces, rubs and seasonings are made using staples I have on hand in my home kitchen. I have deliberately kept these basic to encourage you to experiment and become an expert at combining your own flavours.

Please feel free to adapt all of the recipes in this book as you see fit. Substitute one animal protein for another – say, replace fish with chicken, or beef with lamb and so on – and add or remove a sauce or spice rub. Basically, the idea is to free flow and do whatever makes you happy and tastes good.

It's that simple.

> It is always a joy for me to bring together a great bunch of recipes that, from the first bite to the last, inspire and bring smiles to people's faces.

As with my previous books written over nearly a decade, these recipes are based on paleo and keto foundations, and are all dairy, grain and legume free. Not only do these principles work well for our bodies and minds, but our planet also benefits in many ways. I always steer well clear of processed foods and foods that can most commonly cause inflammation – grains, legumes and dairy. Instead, I eat good-quality proteins and fats from well-sourced land and sea animals, adding some low-carb vegetables as well as fermented foods and bone broths made from organic ingredients whenever possible. I've been road-testing the low-carb, healthy fats lifestyle for a number of years now and I find the more consistent I am with what and when I eat, the more energy I have to live my life.

When choosing animal proteins and fats, go for organic, free-range, pasture-raised or grass-fed-and-finished meat or wild game and sustainable wild-caught seafood. And when it comes to fruit, vegetables and herbs, choose organic and spray free or, best of all, home grown wherever possible. I use either coconut oil or good-quality animal fats for cooking as they have high smoke points (meaning they do not oxidise at high temperatures). Some of my favourite animal fats are lard (pork fat), tallow (rendered beef fat), rendered chicken fat and duck fat. Ask for them at your butcher, look online for meat suppliers who sell them or make your own when making bone broths.

Apart from that, preparing the perfect meal really is as straightforward as putting well-sourced meat, seafood or eggs on your plate, along with some healthy fat, and adding some cooked vegetables or a salad on the side. To provide probiotic gut health goodness, I also love to include condiments such as fermented vegetables – think sauerkraut or kimchi – on the table at every meal.

I hope these recipes become favourites for you and your loved ones and that you get a lot of pleasure from sharing them. It is always a joy for me to bring together a great bunch of recipes that, from the first bite to the last, inspire and bring smiles to people's faces.

It is my hope that *Dinner in 5* will become the new go-to cookbook for health-minded families everywhere. It is all about paring things back to the bare essentials: just a handful of simple, commonly used ingredients can create a delicious and memorable meal. What could be better?

Keep cooking with love and laughter,

EGGS

MUSHROOMS AND EGG ON TOAST WITH PESTO

SERVES 4

swiss brown mushrooms 8, sliced
eggs 4
paleo bread 4 slices, toasted
+
coconut oil or good-quality animal fat
   3 tablespoons
sea salt and freshly ground black pepper
pesto 75 g (page 239) (optional)

Mushrooms on toast is one of my all-time favourite meals as it's so quick to whip up. Adding a fried egg makes a hearty meal that can be enjoyed for breakfast, lunch or dinner. The flavour of the runny yolk is perfect with the earthy mushrooms and a dollop of quick cheat's pesto really rounds out the dish. You can have this on the table in less than 10 minutes if you have some grain- and gluten-free paleo bread on hand.

Heat 2 tablespoons of the coconut oil or fat in a large frying pan over medium heat. Add the mushrooms and sauté for 3–4 minutes until cooked through and starting to colour. Season with salt and pepper.

Heat the remaining coconut oil or fat in a large non-stick frying pan over medium heat. Crack in the eggs and fry until the whites are set and the yolks are cooked to your liking, 2 ½–3 minutes for soft egg yolks. Season with salt and pepper.

Place a slice of toast on each plate, spoon over the mushrooms, top with a fried egg and finish with a drizzle of pesto. Serve with the remaining pesto on the side.

EGG SALAD WITH PICKLES AND CHIVES

SERVES 2

eggs 4
cornichons 3–4, finely sliced
chives 1 small handful, finely snipped
+
mayonnaise 3 tablespoons (page 237)
sea salt and freshly ground black pepper

This delicious dish can be eaten as a salad on its own, on some toasted paleo bread or enjoyed as part of a larger meal alongside a burger patty, a fillet of fish or some other meat. It is based on the classic French sauce called gribiche, which is made up of chopped hard-boiled eggs, cornichons, herbs and, to bind everything together, mayonnaise. Delicious!

Fill a saucepan with water and bring to the boil. Turn down the heat to medium–low, add the eggs and cook for 6 minutes for semi-soft-boiled eggs (or cook to your liking). Immediately transfer the eggs to ice-cold water to stop the cooking process. Once the eggs have cooled, peel under cold running water and cut into quarters lengthways.

Place the egg, cornichons and chives in a serving bowl. Add the mayonnaise and gently mix through. Season with salt and pepper and serve.

pepper

NIC'S AVOCADO TOAST WITH POACHED EGGS

SERVES 4

avocados 2, diced
white or apple cider vinegar 80 ml (⅓ cup)
eggs 8
paleo bread 8 slices, toasted
+
south american dressing 150 ml (page 242)
sea salt and freshly ground black pepper

My wife Nic makes the most awesome paleo and keto breads and she never follows a recipe – she just freestyles. She loves to use her breads in as many different ways as possible, and it is hard to beat a good old avo toast with poached eggs. We are lucky enough to have our own chickens that produce the most beautiful eggs for us.

Place the avocado and 3 tablespoons of the dressing in a bowl, crush lightly with a fork, then mix to combine. Season with salt and pepper.

Meanwhile, pour the vinegar into a saucepan of boiling salted water, then reduce the heat to medium–low so the water is just simmering. Crack an egg into a cup. Using a wooden spoon, stir the simmering water in one direction to form a whirlpool and drop the egg into the centre. Repeat with the remaining eggs and cook for 3 minutes for runny yolks, or cook to your liking. Remove the eggs with a slotted spoon and place on paper towel to drain.

To serve, spread the avocado over the toast, then top with a poached egg. Drizzle over the remaining dressing and finish with a sprinkle of salt and pepper.

Tip: Add a little smoked trout to this dish, if you fancy.

BACON AND EGG TOASTED SANGA

SERVES 4

rindless bacon 8 rashers
eggs 4
paleo bread 8 slices, toasted
+
coconut oil or good-quality animal fat
   2 tablespoons
sea salt and freshly ground black pepper
mayonnaise 80 g (page 237)

Okay, now we're getting serious ... well, as serious as a bacon and egg sanga can get. I have used paleo bread so those avoiding gluten or grains can chow down on this quintessential Aussie breakfast. There is nothing fancy about this sandwich – simply cook the bacon and eggs to your liking, toast the bread and spread with your favourite sauce. This also makes for a pretty impressive school or work lunch.

Heat half the coconut oil or fat in a large frying pan over medium–high heat. Add the bacon and pan-fry, turning occasionally, for 3–5 minutes until golden and crisp (or cook to your liking). Remove from the pan, drain on paper towel and keep warm.

Wipe the pan clean with paper towel, place over medium–high heat and add the remaining coconut oil or fat. (Or just crack the eggs straight into the bacon fat like I do!) Crack in the eggs and fry until the whites are set and the yolks are cooked to your liking, 2 ½–3 minutes for soft egg yolks. Season with salt and pepper to taste.

Spread half the mayonnaise on four slices of toast, then top each slice with two rashers of bacon and a fried egg. Spread a little more mayonnaise on the remaining slices of toast and place on the egg and bacon to form a sandwich. Serve while still hot.

SOFT-BOILED EGGS WITH ANCHOVIES AND CAPERS

SERVES 4

eggs 4
salted anchovy fillets 16, rinsed and
    patted dry
salted baby capers 40 g (¼ cup), rinsed
    and patted dry
+
mayonnaise 80 g (page 237)
chervil sprigs to serve
extra-virgin olive oil or truffle olive oil
    for drizzling
sea salt and freshly ground black pepper

Egg salads should never be underestimated as a delicious dish to serve for friends or family. I boil up half a dozen or so eggs during the week, so I always have them on hand when I want to whip up a quick meal. The addition of anchovies and capers may not be to everyone's liking, but for me this combination hits the spot every time. You can swap the anchovies for prawns, smoked fish or roast chicken if you prefer.

Fill a saucepan with water and bring to the boil. Turn down the heat to medium–low, add the eggs and cook for 4 ½ minutes for soft-boiled eggs (or cook to your liking). Immediately transfer the eggs to ice-cold water to stop the cooking process. Once the eggs have cooled, peel under cold running water and cut in half lengthways.

Dollop and smear the mayonnaise on four small serving plates. Divide the eggs, anchovies and capers among the plates. Serve with the chervil, a drizzle of olive oil or truffle oil and a sprinkle of salt and pepper over the eggs.

SCRAMBLED EGGS WITH MUSHROOMS AND SILVERBEET

SERVES 2

portobello mushrooms 4, cleaned
silverbeet leaves 2, stems removed (reserve
   for making bone broth), roughly chopped
eggs 4
+
coconut oil or good-quality animal fat
   2 ½ tablespoons, melted
sea salt and freshly ground black pepper

Scrambled eggs are a lifesaver when you want to whip up a quick meal. To round them out, I love to add something simple, as I have done here with mushrooms and greens. If you want to include some meat, then steak, sausages, bacon or a lovely piece of wild salmon are all great additions.

Preheat the oven to 180°C (160°C fan-forced).

Place the mushrooms on a baking tray, drizzle on 1 tablespoon of the coconut oil or fat and season with salt and pepper. Roast for 10–15 minutes until the mushrooms are soft and juicy.

Meanwhile, heat 2 teaspoons of the coconut oil or fat in a frying pan over medium heat, add the silverbeet and cook until it is wilted, 1–2 minutes. Season with salt and pepper. Set aside, keeping warm.

To make the scrambled eggs, crack the eggs into a bowl and beat with a fork until smooth. Season with salt and pepper. Melt the remaining 1 tablespoon of coconut oil or fat in a non-stick frying pan over medium–low heat. Pour in the egg mixture and stir gently with a wooden spoon until the eggs are just set, 1 ½–2 minutes.

Divide the scrambled eggs, mushrooms and silverbeet between two plates and serve with extra pepper sprinkled over the top.

FRIED EGGS WITH JAMON AND ASPARAGUS

SERVES 4

eggs 4
asparagus 2 bunches (about 300 g),
    trimmed and cut in half lengthways
serrano jamon (or prosciutto) 8 slices
+
coconut oil or good-quality animal fat
    2 tablespoons
sea salt and freshly ground black pepper
extra-virgin olive oil for drizzling
chopped flat-leaf parsley leaves to serve

I love dishes you can throw together in a matter of minutes, and this is one such recipe. Simply combine a fried egg with some charred asparagus to create something truly special. I am a huge fan of jamon, a Spanish ham similar to Italian prosciutto, so I've added that here, but feel free to use whatever you have on hand. Bacon works well or you could include some smoked trout.

Heat 1 tablespoon of the coconut oil or fat in a large non-stick frying pan over medium heat. Crack in the eggs and fry until the whites are set and the yolks are cooked to your liking, 2 ½–3 minutes for soft egg yolks. Season with salt and pepper. Slide the eggs onto a plate and keep warm.

Heat the remaining coconut oil or fat in a large frying pan over medium–high heat. Add the asparagus and cook, turning occasionally, for 3–3 ½ minutes until lightly charred and cooked through but still slightly crunchy in the centre. Season with salt and pepper.

Arrange the asparagus on four plates, then add a fried egg and two slices of jamon. Drizzle over some olive oil, scatter on the parsley and sprinkle with some pepper to serve.

COS LETTUCE WITH BACON AND EGGS

SERVES 4

eggs 6, at room temperature
rindless bacon 6 rashers
baby cos lettuces 2, leaves separated
    and torn
+
coconut oil or good-quality animal fat
    2 teaspoons
caesar dressing 100 g (page 230)
sea salt and freshly ground black pepper

This is my very simple take on the world-famous Caesar salad. Yes, I have taken a few short cuts to get a quick and tasty salad on the table using just cos lettuce, boiled eggs, crispy bacon and a mayo dressing. If you want to go traditional, add some anchovies and croutons, but I think this fits the bill perfectly for a weeknight salad to serve alongside some fish, chicken or steak.

Fill a saucepan with water and bring to the boil. Turn down the heat to medium–low, add the eggs and simmer for 6 minutes for semi-soft-boiled eggs (or cook to your liking). Immediately transfer the eggs to ice-cold water to stop the cooking process. Once the eggs have cooled, peel under cold running water and cut in half lengthways.

Heat the coconut oil or fat in a large frying pan over medium heat. Add the bacon and pan-fry, turning occasionally, until golden and crisp, about 2 minutes on each side. Remove from the pan and drain on paper towel. When cool enough to handle, chop the bacon into small pieces.

Arrange the cos leaves in a large shallow serving bowl, top with the bacon and egg and drizzle over the dressing. Season with salt and pepper and serve.

HAM AND SPINACH OMELETTE

SERVES 2–4

eggs 6 large
ham 150 g thinly sliced, torn
baby spinach leaves 50 g (2 cups),
    stems removed
+
sea salt and freshly ground black pepper
coconut oil or good-quality animal fat
    2 tablespoons

Few things are easier to cook than a simple and elegant one-pan omelette. This type of cooking is what I love most, as you basically mix it up and then set and forget for 15 minutes. You can pretty much put anything into these omelettes. Add some seafood, leftover meat or smallgoods, such as pasture-raised ham, and any type of veg you feel like. These are my go-to for family breakfasts and are fantastic for school lunches, too.

Crack the eggs into a bowl, lightly beat with a fork and season with salt and pepper.

Heat the coconut oil or fat in a 24 cm non-stick ovenproof frying pan over medium heat. Add the ham and pan-fry for 2 minutes. Reduce the heat to low, scatter over the spinach, pour on the egg mixture and gently fold through. Cook for 5–10 minutes to set the base and side.

Meanwhile, preheat the grill to medium.

Place the omelette under the grill for 3–3 ½ minutes until the top is lightly golden and set. Serve.

SEAFOOD

PAN-FRIED SNAPPER WITH SAUCE VIERGE

SERVES 4

fresh or frozen peas 100 g
green beans 120 g, trimmed
snapper fillets 4 x 180 g, pin-boned, skin on
+
sea salt and freshly ground black pepper
coconut oil or good-quality animal fat
    2 tablespoons
sauce vierge 380 g (page 242)
lemon wedges to serve

Just looking at this dish makes me happy. A simple tomato dressing with some greens and crispy skin fish is just the ticket when it comes to a quick and healthy weeknight dinner for the whole family. I often cook this as I know I can have it ready in 10–15 minutes. You could replace the fish with any meat you like.

Blanch the peas in boiling salted water for 3 minutes, or until just tender. Remove with a slotted spoon and plunge into ice-cold water. Drain and set aside. Using the same boiling water, blanch the beans for 2 minutes, or until just tender. Again, plunge into ice-cold water, then drain and set aside.

Season the snapper fillets with salt and pepper.

Heat the coconut oil or fat in a large heavy-based frying pan over high heat. Add the snapper, skin-side down, and fry for 2½–3 minutes until crispy. Flip the fish and cook for 2 minutes, or until the fish is just cooked through. Transfer to a plate and allow to rest for 2 minutes, keeping warm.

Meanwhile, place the sauce vierge in a saucepan over medium heat. Add the peas and beans and cook for 3 minutes, or until heated through.

Divide the peas and beans among serving plates, top with a fish fillet, spoon over the sauce vierge and serve with a lemon wedge on the side. Or serve it all in one large dish for sharing at the table.

SMOKED TROUT WITH CUCUMBER AND DILL

This has to be the easiest and quickest dish in this whole cookbook – from start to finish, it can be on the table in 5 minutes. All you need to have on hand is good-quality smoked fish, cucumber, dill and mayonnaise. If you want to add a little more sustenance, then you could serve it with some boiled eggs.

Finely shave one cucumber into ribbons using a mandoline or peeler, then finely slice the other cucumber into rounds.

Smear the mayonnaise over two serving plates, top with the smoked trout, cucumber and dill, drizzle on the olive oil and finish with a good grind of pepper.

SERVES 2

lebanese cucumbers 2
smoked trout 1 whole (about 250 g), flesh flaked
dill fronds 1 large handful
+
mayonnaise 100 g (page 237)
extra-virgin olive oil for drizzling
freshly ground black pepper

DORY WITH OLIVES AND SILVERBEET

SERVES 4

silver dory fillets 4 x 140–160 g (or any
   white-flesh fish), skin on
lemons 2, cut into cheeks
garlic cloves 6, finely chopped
silverbeet 12 leaves, stems removed (reserve
   for making bone broth), roughly chopped
kalamata olives 115 g (¾ cup), pitted
+
sea salt and freshly ground black pepper
**melted coconut oil or good-quality
   animal fat** 80 ml (⅓ cup)
extra-virgin olive oil for drizzling

I don't really need to say too much about this dish
except … cook it!

Season the dory fillets with salt and pepper.

Heat 2 tablespoons of the coconut oil or fat in a non-stick frying
pan over high heat. Add the fish and fry for 1 ½ minutes on each
side, or until crispy and golden and cooked through. Remove
from the pan and squeeze over about 2 teaspoons of juice from
the lemon cheeks.

Meanwhile, heat the remaining 2 tablespoons of coconut oil
or fat in the same pan over medium heat, add the garlic and
cook, stirring occasionally, for 1 minute, or until fragrant. Add
the silverbeet and 3 tablespoons of water and sauté until the
silverbeet is wilted, 2–3 minutes. Stir in the olives and sauté for
a further 1 minute, or until heated through. Season with salt and
pepper. Set aside, keeping warm.

Place the fish on serving plates, add the silverbeet and olives
and drizzle over some olive oil. Serve with a lemon cheek on
the side.

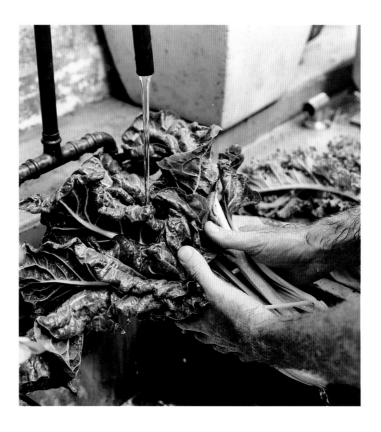

GARLIC PRAWNS

raw king prawns 16, deveined
lemon 1, cut in half
+
melted coconut oil or good-quality animal fat for brushing

Garlic dressing
coconut oil or good-quality animal fat 1 tablespoon, melted
garlic cloves 8, finely chopped
extra-virgin olive oil 100 ml
chilli flakes ½–1 teaspoon (optional)
sea salt and freshly ground black pepper

I am a huge fan of eating food with my hands and it doesn't get much better than prawns in their shells. I simply barbecue or chargrill the prawns so the shells are lovely and charred and the flesh is nice and juicy. A squeeze of lemon and a sprinkle of salt is all that is needed for a perfect weekend barbecue. If you want to get a little fancy, add a delicious garlic dressing like the one here.

Soak 16 bamboo skewers in cold water for 20 minutes (or use metal ones). Drain.

To make the dressing, heat the coconut oil or fat in a saucepan over medium heat. Add the garlic and cook for 1–1 ½ minutes, or until softened, fragrant and just starting to colour. Transfer the garlic to a bowl, then whisk in the olive oil. Season with the chilli flakes (if using) and salt and pepper. Set aside until needed.

Starting at the tail end, thread each prawn onto a skewer, then brush with the coconut oil or fat.

Heat a barbecue grill plate to hot or a large chargrill pan over high heat. Add the prawn skewers and cook for 1–2 minutes on each side until the prawns are charred and cooked through. Add the lemon halves, flesh-side down, and cook for 2 minutes, or until charred.

Season the prawns with salt and pepper.

To serve, place the skewers on a platter, drizzle the garlic dressing over the prawns, then add a good squeeze of charred lemon.

STEAMED SALMON WITH SPRING ONIONS AND GINGER

I adore the flavours in Chinese cooking. Seafood is treated with the greatest of care and the ingredients absolutely shine. Ginger and spring onion is a classic combination, so I have used them in this dish, which offers so much in terms of taste. Usually, this is made with a white-flesh fish, but I love it with wild salmon or trout.

Season the salmon with salt and pepper.

Line a steamer basket with a sheet of baking paper. Fill a saucepan with water, bring to the boil, then reduce the heat to low. Place the salmon in the steamer, cover and steam for 3–4 minutes until the fish is still a slightly deeper pink in the centre and almost cooked through. Transfer to a plate and allow to rest for 2 minutes, keeping warm.

Meanwhile, combine the broth, spring onion and ginger in a saucepan and place over medium–low heat. Bring to a gentle simmer and cook for 5 minutes, or until the spring onion is tender. If needed, season with a little salt.

To serve, ladle the broth, spring onion and ginger into warm serving bowls. Add the steamed salmon fillets, then finish with the extra ginger and micro coriander (if using).

SERVES 4

salmon fillets 4 x 150 g, skin on, pin-boned
chinese broth 700 ml (page 231)
spring onions 8, white and green parts cut into 8 cm lengths
ginger 6 cm piece, cut into matchsticks, plus extra to serve
+
sea salt and freshly ground black pepper
micro coriander leaves to serve (optional)

WHOLE SARDINES WITH SPINACH, LEMON AND GARLIC

This might just be my favourite recipe in this whole book for a few reasons. First, it uses a sustainable seafood that offers us a great deal of health benefits. Second, sardines are so yummy. (If you don't like their taste, I encourage you to slowly start adding one here or there to develop your palate and appreciation for them. Trust me, I was the fussiest eater but I trained myself to love them – and oysters, offal and other foods I initially found unappealing.) Third, it is such a quick dish to put together and can be on the table in a matter of minutes.

Heat 1 tablespoon of the coconut oil or fat in a large non-stick frying pan over medium–high heat. Add the sardines in batches and cook for 30 seconds on each side, or until cooked through. Transfer to a plate and allow to rest for 2 minutes, keeping warm.

Wipe the pan clean with paper towel and place over medium–high heat. Add the remaining coconut oil or fat, then add the garlic and cook for 1 minute, or until fragrant and starting to colour. Next, add the spinach and sauté for 2 minutes, or until just wilted. Season with salt and pepper.

Arrange the spinach and sardines on a platter. Drizzle over the olive oil and lemon juice, sprinkle on the lemon zest and serve with the lemon wedges.

Tip: Mayonnaise (page 237) or romesco sauce (page 241) go well with this dish.

SERVES 4

sardines 12 whole, cleaned, scaled and gutted (ask your fishmonger to do this)
garlic cloves 6, finely sliced
english spinach 1 bunch (about 300 g), trimmed
lemon 1 (finely grated zest and juice of ½, other ½ cut into wedges)
+
coconut oil or good-quality animal fat 3 tablespoons
sea salt and freshly ground black pepper
extra-virgin olive oil 2 tablespoons

PRAWNS WITH CHORIZO AND ROMESCO SAUCE

SERVES 4

raw king prawns 12
chorizo sausages 2, sliced
baby rocket leaves 2 large handfuls
+
coconut oil or good-quality animal fat
   3 tablespoons, melted
sea salt and freshly ground black pepper
romesco sauce 225 g (page 241)
extra-virgin olive oil for drizzling
lemon wedges to serve

A summer salad can be as simple as popping freshly cooked prawns in a bowl and adding a delicious dressing and some leaves. Here, I have taken my inspiration from Spain and included grilled chorizo – so we have a surf and turf theme going on – and a romesco sauce, which works beautifully to bring all the ingredients together. No time to make the romesco sauce? Use mayo or any other dressing in this book that takes your fancy.

To butterfly the prawns, cut along the back from the base of the head to the tip of the tail. Leave the legs connected, remove and discard the vein.

Heat a barbecue grill plate to hot or a chargrill pan over high heat. Brush the prawns with 1 tablespoon of the coconut oil or fat and season with salt and pepper. Cook the prawns for 40–60 seconds on each side until just cooked through. Set aside, keeping warm.

Heat the remaining coconut oil or fat in a frying pan over medium–high heat. Add the chorizo and cook, turning regularly, for 3 minutes, or until browned.

Divide and arrange the rocket, chorizo, romesco sauce and prawns among four serving bowls. Drizzle over some olive oil and serve with lemon wedges to squeeze over the top.

SNAPPER WITH HEALING SPICES AND GREENS

SERVES 2–4

snapper fillets 4 x 120 g, skin on or off
asparagus 2 bunches (about 300 g),
    woody ends trimmed
watercress sprigs 1 large handful

+

olive oil 3 tablespoons, plus extra
    for drizzling
healing spice blend 1 ½ teaspoons
    (page 220)
sea salt and freshly ground black pepper
lemon wedges to serve
mayonnaise 80 g (page 237)

To take a dish from plain to sublime, coat a piece of fish or meat in a spice rub or marinade – this is such a simple thing and brings so much flavour. I love this healing spice blend and use it often in my home cooking, as it goes beautifully with chicken, pork, lamb, prawns and fish. It is that good – all you need to add are some fresh greens and a little mayonnaise for good measure.

Preheat the oven to 170°C (150°C fan-forced). Line a baking tray with baking paper.

Combine the olive oil and spice blend in a bowl and mix well.

Place the fish fillets on the prepared tray, spoon the spice oil over the fish to completely coat both sides, then season with pepper. Roast for 6–8 minutes until the fish is cooked through. Transfer to a plate and allow to rest for 2 minutes, keeping warm.

Meanwhile, blanch the asparagus in salted boiling water for 3 minutes, or until just tender. Drain, then drizzle over a little olive oil and sprinkle on some salt and pepper if needed.

Arrange the asparagus on serving plates, add the watercress and fish and serve with the lemon wedges and mayo on the side.

SPAGHETTI BOLOGNESE WITH A TWIST

SERVES 4

italian tomato sauce 700 g (page 236)
white-flesh fish fillets (such as snapper or barramundi) 400 g, skin off, pin-boned and finely chopped
butternut pumpkin 600 g, spiralised into thin noodles
oregano leaves 1 small handful

+

sea salt and freshly ground black pepper
extra-virgin olive oil for drizzling

This is my take on the classic spaghetti bolognese. Instead of using minced meat, I simmer finely chopped fish in a tomato sauce until it's moist, juicy and full of flavour. I also replace the traditional pasta with pumpkin spaghetti, as I find this adds more intensity, but feel free to use whatever noodle or vegetable you love. I encourage you to try this dish and discover just how yummy it is.

Place the tomato sauce in a saucepan and bring to a simmer over medium heat. Reduce the heat to medium–low, stir in the fish and cook for 8 minutes, or until the fish is cooked through. Season with salt and pepper.

Meanwhile, bring a saucepan of salted water to the boil. Add the pumpkin spaghetti and cook for 30 seconds, or until tender. Drain well. Toss the spaghetti with a drizzle of olive oil and season with salt.

Divide the spaghetti among four serving bowls, spoon over the sauce, sprinkle on the oregano and serve.

PRAWN COCKTAIL

SERVES 4

raw king prawns 20
baby cucumbers 8. cut lengthways
　　into wedges
+
lemon wedges to serve
sea salt and freshly ground black pepper
cocktail sauce 300 g (page 232)

I love eating prawn salads in the warmer months, so it's great to have ice-cold cooked prawns on hand to throw together a dish like this. I add whatever vegetable or fruit is in season. In summer, cucumbers are at their peak, making it a no-brainer to combine the two. You could use lettuce as well or a bunch of herbs fresh from the garden. Served alongside is the perfect accompaniment: the classic cocktail sauce. If you have some paleo bread, you can whip up delicious prawn sangas.

Cook the prawns in salted boiling water for 2 ½–3 minutes until pink and firm. Transfer to a bowl of ice-cold water to cool completely. Peel and devein, keeping the tails intact. If you like, you can keep the heads intact too for presentation.

Arrange the prawns, cucumber and lemon wedges on a platter, season with salt and pepper and serve with the cocktail sauce in a dipping bowl on the side.

SLOW-COOKED SALMON WITH JAPANESE SPICES

SERVES 4

salmon fillets 4 x 160 g, skin on
mixed salad leaves 2 handfuls
   (or use seaweed)
daikon ¼, finely grated
+
coconut oil or good-quality animal fat
2 tablespoons, melted
sea salt and freshly ground black pepper
japanese dressing 3 tablespoons (page 236)
japanese spice blend 1 tablespoon
   (page 221)

Sometimes a beautifully cooked piece of fish, served with a sprinkle of spice and a little salad, is all I want for dinner – eating well really doesn't need to be more complicated than that. The beautiful Japanese-inspired spice blend used here lifts the slow-cooked salmon to another level. I encourage you to make some of the spice blends featured in this book and experiment with them – it's such a simple no-fuss way to add depth and flavour to all your dishes.

Preheat the oven to 110°C (90°C fan-forced). Line a baking tray with baking paper.

Coat the salmon with the coconut oil or fat and season with salt and pepper. Place the salmon, skin-side down, on the prepared tray and slowly bake in the oven for 13–16 minutes until medium–rare (or cook to your liking). Transfer to a plate and allow to rest for 2 minutes, keeping warm.

Place the salad leaves in a bowl, add the Japanese dressing and gently toss. Season with salt and pepper if needed.

Arrange the salad on serving plates and top with the salmon. Sprinkle on the Japanese spice blend and serve with the daikon on the side.

PAN-FRIED BLUE MACKEREL WITH CUCUMBER AND RADISH

To create an awesome fish meal, all you need to remember is this: grill or pan-fry the skin until it is lovely and golden and crispy, then season it well with salt. It's also important to know that some fish needs to be just cooked through whereas other types are best lightly seared or undercooked. If you do your research, you really can't go wrong. Add a squeeze of lemon juice and a dollop of mayo, serve with a nice salad and, voila.

Season the mackerel fillets with salt and pepper.

Heat the coconut oil or fat in a large frying pan over high heat. Add the mackerel, skin-side down, and fry for 1 ½ minutes, then flip and cook for 15–20 seconds until the fish is just cooked through and the skin is crispy. Transfer to a plate and allow to rest for 2 minutes, keeping warm.

To serve, spread the mayonnaise on four serving plates and top with the mackerel fillets (three fillets per plate). Scatter over the radish and cucumber, drizzle with a little olive oil, squeeze on some lemon juice and finish with a good grind of pepper.

SERVES 4

blue mackerel fillets 12 x 60–70 g, skin on, pin-boned and halved
radishes 4, finely sliced
lebanese cucumber 1 large, finely sliced
+
sea salt and freshly ground black pepper
coconut oil or good-quality animal fat 3 tablespoons
mayonnaise 100 g (page 237)
extra-virgin olive oil for drizzling
lemon wedges to serve

CLAMS WITH GARLIC, CHILLI AND PARSLEY

SERVES 4

long red chillies 4, halved, deseeded
    and finely chopped
garlic cloves 6, finely chopped
flat-leaf parsley leaves 1 large handful,
    finely chopped
clams 1 kg, soaked in cold water
+
coconut oil or good-quality animal fat
    1 tablespoon
sea salt and freshly ground black pepper
extra-virgin olive oil 3 tablespoons

As a father, my intention is to expose my daughters to a wide range of experiences, especially those that increase their understanding of the world around them. One of the best ways I have found to do this is to expand their palates and introduce new flavours and ingredients by offering foods from around the globe. A couple of years ago, both my girls developed a love for pipis and clams, so every month or so I prepare a simple dish like this. Ready in 10 minutes, this can be enjoyed as a starter, light lunch or main meal.

Heat the coconut oil or fat in a large, heavy-based saucepan over medium heat. Add the chilli and garlic and cook for 1 minute, or until fragrant. Stir in the parsley and cook for 15 seconds, or until softened.

Turn the heat to high, add the clams and 200 ml of water, cover with the lid and cook for 3 minutes, or until the clams have just opened. Transfer the clams to a bowl, discarding any unopened shells.

Bring the liquid in the pan to the boil and cook until reduced by half, 2–3 minutes. Season with salt and pepper and add the olive oil. Return the clams to the pan and serve immediately.

Tip: Adding a little bacon or jamon to this dish is a wonderful way to boost flavour and texture.

SALMON TATAKI

sashimi-grade salmon 400 g
salmon roe 3 heaped tablespoons
baby shiso or coriander leaves
    1 small handful
+
coconut oil 1 tablespoon, melted
sea salt
japanese dressing 140 ml (page 236)
wasabi paste to serve

From time to time I love picking up beautiful fresh fish from the market and serving it sashimi style as an appetiser. My family adores it. You can use any fresh fish or seafood, such as kingfish, ocean trout, salmon, tuna, mackerel, scallops or prawns. Freshly shucked oysters are wonderful, too. Then, simply add this delicious Japanese dressing and, if you like a little spice, some wasabi.

Heat a barbecue hotplate to hot or a heavy-based frying pan over high heat.

Lightly brush the salmon with the coconut oil and season with salt. Sear the fish for 5 seconds on all sides to seal. Allow to cool, then cover and place in the fridge to chill for 1–2 hours.

Using a sharp knife, cut the fish into 5 mm thick slices and arrange on a platter. Spoon over the dressing, then scatter over the salmon roe and shiso or coriander leaves. Serve with the wasabi on the side.

OYSTERS WITH JAMON VINAIGRETTE

It isn't often I feature oysters in my cookbooks because I do love them plain, but every now and then I like to play around with different toppings. This vinaigrette is a beauty that works equally well as a dressing for barbecued fish, scallops or prawns. If you want to cook your oysters, then you could pop some vinaigrette on top before you cook them or try spooning some over after cooking.

To make the vinaigrette, place the shallot, jamon, vinegar, olive oil and chives in a bowl and mix to combine. Season with salt and pepper.

Arrange the oysters on a platter of ice and top each one with a spoonful of vinaigrette.

SERVES 4

oysters 24, freshly shucked

Jamon Vinaigrette
french shallot 1, finely chopped
serrano jamon (or prosciutto) 80 g, finely diced
red wine vinegar 80 ml (⅓ cup)
extra-virgin olive oil 80 ml (⅓ cup)
finely snipped chives 1 teaspoon
sea salt and freshly ground black pepper

SARDINES ON TOAST

SERVES 4

truss or roma tomatoes 6, cut in half

paleo bread 8 slices

whole sardines 12, cleaned, scaled and gutted (ask your fishmonger to do this)

+

coconut oil or good-quality animal fat 2 tablespoons, melted

sea salt and freshly ground black pepper

garlic-infused olive oil or extra-virgin olive oil for drizzling

Over the years on my travels through Spain, *pan con tomate* – basically crushed tomato on toast with a hint (or a lot!) of garlic to intensify the flavour – has remained a favourite dish. Here, I use gluten- and grain-free bread and include sardines, as I love the combination of sardines, tomato and toast. A good drizzle of olive oil over the top is just what the doctor ordered.

Preheat the oven to 200°C (180°C fan-forced). Heat a barbecue grill plate to hot or a chargrill pan over high heat.

Brush the tomato halves with some of the coconut oil or fat and season with salt and pepper. Cook the tomato halves for 1 minute on each side, or until charred. Transfer to a baking tray and bake for 8 minutes, or until soft. Place in a bowl and crush with a fork until chunky. Set aside, keeping warm.

Next, chargrill the bread on both sides until crisp, about 1–1 ½ minutes. Drizzle over the olive oil and set aside.

Brush the sardines with the remaining coconut oil or fat and chargrill for 40 seconds on each side, or until cooked through.

To serve, spread the crushed tomato on the chargrilled bread, then top with the sardines. Season with some extra salt and pepper and drizzle with a little more olive oil.

FRIED BLUE MACKEREL WITH CRISPY GARLIC AND CHILLI

SERVES 4

blue mackerel fillets 12 x 60–70 g, skin on, pin-boned
tapioca flour 150 g (see note)
garlic cloves 8, finely chopped
long red chillies 2, finely sliced
+
sea salt and freshly ground black pepper
coconut oil or good-quality animal fat for deep-frying
coriander leaves to serve
lime wedges to serve (optional)

Is it any wonder that fried fish is so popular? That delicate, moist and flaky flesh with its lovely crispy outer crust needs nothing more than a squeeze of citrus juice. Yum! In this recipe I have given it a healthy twist and used mackerel, with garlic, chilli and coriander added for flavour. Enjoy!

Season the mackerel fillets with salt and pepper, then dust with the tapioca flour.

Heat the coconut oil or fat to 160°C in a wok or large saucepan. (To test the temperature, drop a small piece of fish into the oil – it should bubble instantly around the edges.) Working in batches, fry the fish for 60–90 seconds, or until cooked through. Drain on paper towel and season with more salt and pepper if needed. Set aside, keeping warm.

Reheat the oil or fat in the wok or pan to 160°C. Add the garlic and chilli and fry for 20–30 seconds, or until the garlic is pale golden and crispy. (The garlic can burn very quickly so remove the pan from the heat as soon as it turns pale golden.) Strain the garlic and chilli (reserve the oil for other dishes, such as the sardines on toast on page 65), then carefully shake off the excess oil. Drain on paper towel and season with salt.

Arrange the fish on a platter, sprinkle over the garlic and chilli, scatter over the coriander and serve with the lime wedges, if using.

Note: Tapioca flour is made by grinding up the dried root of the manioc (also known as cassava) plant. It can be used to thicken dishes or in gluten-free baking. You can find tapioca flour at health-food stores and some supermarkets.

Tip: Mayonnaise (page 237) is an awesome addition to this dish.

FISH IN A BAG

SERVES 2

whole snappers 2 x 1 kg, cleaned, scaled and
    gutted (ask your fishmonger to do this)
lemons 2
garlic bulbs 2, halved horizontally
thyme sprigs 20
+
sea salt and freshly ground black pepper
extra-virgin olive oil 100 ml
herb sauce 125 ml (½ cup) (page 234)

Wrapping whole fish in baking paper, as is often
done in Europe, is a really beautiful way to infuse
flavours into the flesh. Then when you open the bag
at the table, an aromatic cloud of steam is released
to prepare you for the taste sensation you are
about to enjoy. Add this herb sauce and you can
imagine yourself sitting in a cliff-top restaurant
in Italy.

Preheat the oven to 220°C (200°C fan-forced).

Place two sheets of baking paper (each piece should be
large enough to enclose a whole fish) side by side in a large
roasting tin.

Season each fish with salt and pepper, then place in the centre
of a piece of baking paper. Cut one of the lemons into slices
then stuff into each cavity along with the garlic and thyme, then
drizzle over the olive oil. Fold the paper over the fish to form a
package, then fold in the ends to seal. Bake for 18–20 minutes
until each fish is cooked through.

Place each snapper in a bag on a serving plate, open and drizzle
over the herb sauce. Cut the remaining lemon into wedges and
serve on the side.

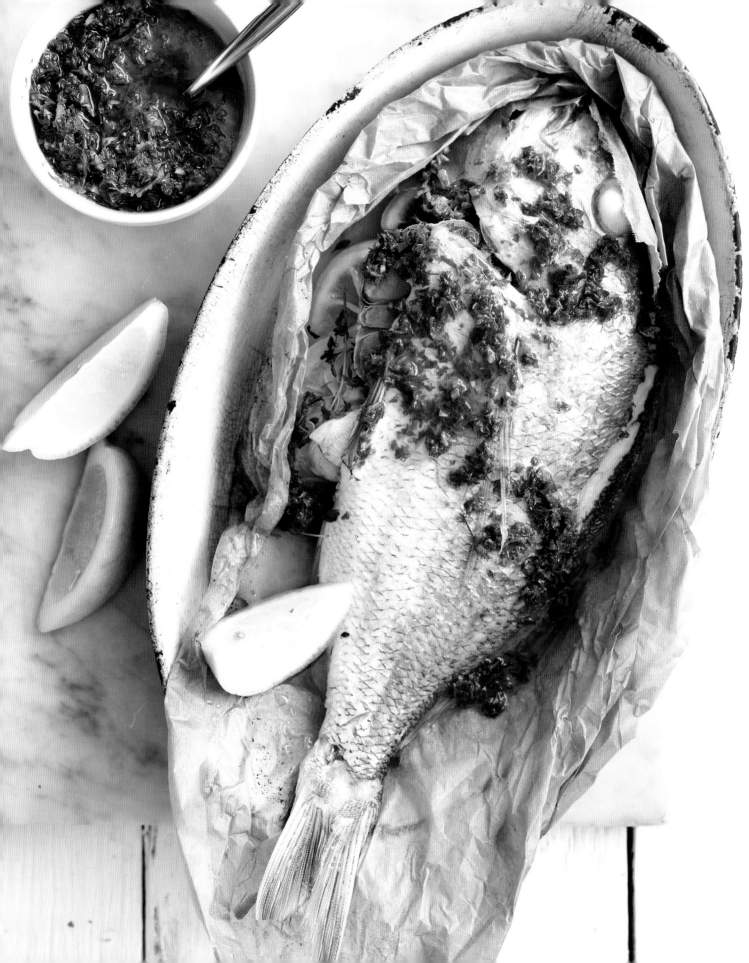

PRAWN EGG FOO YUNG

SERVES 2–4

raw prawns 200 g, peeled and deveined
garlic cloves 2, crushed
eggs 6
shiitake mushrooms 6, sliced
spring onions 2, cut into matchsticks
+
sea salt and freshly ground black pepper
chinese dressing 150 ml (page 232)
coconut oil or good-quality animal fat
2 tablespoons

I ate some wonderful food with my family when we were recently travelling in Japan. Funnily enough, my wife and I ended up eating one meal in a Chinese restaurant in a basement in Tokyo. One of the dishes we ordered was egg foo yung, an omelette with crab, which was simply divine. I wanted to recreate it for you and, here, have used prawns instead – as they are a little more accessible – but by all means feel free to replace them with crab, sea urchin or lobster.

Using a sharp knife, butterfly the prawns by cutting along the back of each prawn. Place the prawns in a bowl, add the garlic and mix well. Cover and marinate in the fridge for 1 hour.

Crack the eggs into a bowl and beat with a fork. Season with salt and pepper.

Pour the Chinese dressing into a saucepan, place over medium heat and bring to a simmer. Season with a little salt and pepper if needed. Set aside, keeping warm.

Heat a large frying pan over medium heat, add the coconut oil or fat and swirl around the pan to coat the base. Add the mushroom and cook for 2 minutes, or until almost cooked through. Stir in the prawns and garlic and cook for 1 minute, or until the garlic is fragrant and the prawns are just starting to change colour. Season with salt and pepper.

Reduce the heat to medium–low. Pour the beaten egg into the pan and swirl to cover the base. Cook, gently pushing the egg mixture from the outside of the pan into the centre, for 30 seconds, then continue to cook undisturbed for 2–3 minutes until set on the underside but still slightly runny on top. Remove from the heat, pour on the Chinese dressing, then scatter over the spring onion. Serve immediately.

LIVER ON TOAST

SERVES 4

john dory livers 600 g (or use chicken
    or beef livers or lamb kidneys)
garlic cloves 4, finely sliced
flat-leaf parsley leaves 1 large handful
red wine vinegar 1 tablespoon
paleo bread 8 slices, toasted
+
sea salt and freshly ground black pepper
coconut oil or good-quality animal fat
    2 tablespoons, plus extra if needed
olive oil 80 ml (⅓ cup)

My dear friend Josh Niland is my favourite seafood chef in the world. I encourage you to visit his Sydney restaurant Saint Peter, where he focuses on nose-to-tail seafood and uses the whole fish, including the liver, blood, heart and everything else, too! I tried his dish of pan-fried john dory liver on toast and thought it so sensational I have attempted to recreate it here. You can, of course, use chicken or beef liver or lamb kidneys as a substitute, or even bone marrow or raw tuna if you prefer.

Season the livers with salt and pepper.

Heat the coconut oil or fat in a large frying pan over medium–high heat. Add the livers, in batches of about four at a time, and cook, for 1–1½ minutes. Flip and cook for another 1–2 minutes until still slightly pink in the centre (or cook to your liking). Transfer to a plate and allow to rest for 2 minutes, keeping warm. Season the livers with salt and pepper.

Add a little more coconut oil or fat to the same pan if needed and reduce the heat to medium. Add the garlic and cook for 40 seconds–1 minute, or until just golden. Remove from the heat and stir in the olive oil, parsley and vinegar. Season with salt and pepper.

To serve, place two slices of toast on each serving plate. Top with the liver, then spoon over the warm garlic and parsley dressing.

CEVICHE WITH AVOCADO AND RADISH

SERVES 4

sashimi-grade kingfish or tuna, spanish mackerel or snapper 600 g, cut in half lengthways
small red onion ¼, finely sliced
avocado 1, diced
radishes 8, finely sliced into rounds
lime ½
+
fine sea salt 2 tablespoons
south american dressing 200 ml (page 242)
finely chopped coriander leaves to serve
freshly ground black pepper

If you catch your own seafood or have access to spanking fresh fish from your fishmonger, you can't go past eating it raw. You can make sashimi, crudo or ceviche like this. I have added avocado, as I love the creaminess it brings to this dish, and radish, as it is so refreshing and gives a beautiful mouthfeel. Drizzle with this easy dressing to tie it all together.

Place the fish on a tray, sprinkle the salt over the flesh, cover and transfer to the fridge to cure for 2 hours.

Scrape the salt off the fish and pat dry with paper towel. Cut the fish into slices about 3 mm thick.

Arrange the fish on a platter or serving plates, scatter over the onion, then drizzle on the dressing and allow to stand for 5 minutes.

To serve, scatter the avocado and radish over the fish, squeeze over the lime juice and sprinkle on the coriander and pepper.

BARBECUED SQUID WITH CUCUMBER AND CORIANDER

Grilled squid can be on the table in a matter of minutes, making it the perfect healthy fast food. You can buy the squid whole and clean it yourself (check out YouTube for some great videos), or buy it already cleaned from your fishmonger so all you need to do is give it a little score with a knife, which helps to tenderise the flesh and capture the flavours of the wonderful sauce that accompanies it. This dish is sensational for a weekend barbecue. Simply prepare your salad ingredients and toss everything together at the last minute. A little green papaya or mango would also be an excellent addition.

Season the squid with salt and pepper.

Heat a barbecue grill plate to medium–hot or a large chargrill pan over medium–high heat. Brush on the coconut oil or fat, add the squid and cook for 1 minute on each side, or until cooked through and lightly charred. Transfer to a plate and allow the squid to cool completely before adding to the salad.

Place the cucumber and radish in a large bowl. Add the squid, pour in the dressing and toss to combine. Transfer to serving bowls, scatter over the coriander and serve.

SERVES 4

baby squid tubes with tentacles 700 g, cleaned, halved lengthways and scored on the inside
lebanese cucumbers 2, finely sliced into rounds
radishes 10, finely sliced into rounds
coriander leaves 1 large handful
+
sea salt and freshly ground black pepper
coconut oil or good-quality animal fat 3 tablespoons, melted
thai dressing 140 ml (page 244)

PAN-FRIED FISH WITH AJI

snapper fillets 4 x 90–130 g, skin on,
   pin-boned
+
sea salt and freshly ground black pepper
coconut oil or good-quality animal fat
   2 tablespoons
lime wedges to serve

Aji
roma tomatoes 4, cut into 1 cm dice
red onion ¼, finely diced (optional)
avocado 1, cut into 1 cm dice
finely chopped coriander leaves
   2 tablespoons, plus extra leaves to serve
sea salt and freshly ground black pepper

Aji is a delicious Colombian sauce that can be served with so many wonderful seafood, meat and vegetable dishes; also try it spooned over salads or as a dipping sauce for empanadas. For this dish, I have teamed it with some superb wild-caught snapper. Have a play and see how you love to serve it.

To make the aji, combine the tomato, red onion (if using), avocado and coriander in a small bowl. Season generously with salt and pepper and let the mixture sit until the salt dissolves, about 2 minutes. Stir in 3 tablespoons of water and set aside.

Season the snapper fillets with salt and pepper.

Heat the coconut oil or fat in a large non-stick frying pan over medium–high heat. Add the snapper, skin-side down, and fry for 2 ½ minutes, or until the skin is golden and crisp. Flip and cook for a further 1 minute, or until just cooked through.

Place the snapper on four serving plates, spoon over the aji, then scatter the extra coriander leaves on top. Serve with the lime wedges.

SALT AND PEPPER PRAWNS

SERVES 4

tapioca flour 100 g, for dusting (see note page 66)
raw king prawns 500 g, halved lengthways with shell intact, deveined
long red chillies 2, finely sliced (optional)
coriander leaves 1 handful
chilli flakes pinch (optional)
+
sea salt and freshly ground black pepper
coconut oil for deep-frying (enough to cover about 6 prawns at a time)
lime wedges to serve

Just because something is deep-fried doesn't mean it is unhealthy, it all depends on two things. First, what is being deep-fried? And second, what oil or fat is being used? I love to use fresh ingredients like seafood and deep-fry it in coconut oil or animal fat (like lard or tallow). Here, in all their goodness, we have salt and pepper prawns that the whole family will adore.

Combine the tapioca flour with a little salt and pepper in a large, shallow bowl. Add half the prawns and toss to coat, shaking off the excess. Repeat with the remaining prawns.

Heat the coconut oil in a wok or large, deep frying pan, add the prawns in batches and deep-fry for 1–2 minutes until they are crispy and golden. Drain on paper towel.

Tip out the coconut oil from the wok or pan and save it to use for another recipe.

Reheat the pan over medium–high heat and add 1 tablespoon of coconut oil back to the pan. Add the fresh chilli (if using) and prawns and gently toss. Add some salt and pepper and continue to toss for 1 minute, or until well combined and the prawns are just cooked through.

To finish, tip the salt and pepper prawns onto a platter and scatter over the coriander leaves. Roughly grind the chilli flakes (if using) with some salt and sprinkle over the prawns. Serve with the lime wedges on the side.

ROAST MACKEREL WITH ENOKI MUSHROOMS AND DAIKON

SERVES 4

blue mackerel fillets 8 x 70–90 g, skin on, pin-boned
enoki mushrooms 300 g, trimmed
daikon 200 g, cut into matchsticks
spring onion 1, cut into matchsticks
+
sea salt and freshly ground black pepper
coconut oil or good-quality animal fat 2 tablespoons, melted
chinese dressing 275 ml (page 232)

The older I get, the more I love oily, strongly flavoured fish like mackerel. I find these types of fish can really handle being paired with bold flavours. You will find mackerel in a lot of Asian dishes, especially curries and soups, as it imparts a richness and umami element that otherwise wouldn't be there. For this recipe, I have teamed the mackerel with mushrooms and daikon, and it is an absolute winner.

Preheat the oven to 120°C (100°C fan-forced). Line a baking tray with baking paper.

Season the mackerel with salt and pepper. Place, skin-side up, on the prepared tray and drizzle over the coconut oil or fat. Roast for 10 minutes, or until the mackerel is just cooked through.

Meanwhile, fill a saucepan with water and place a steamer basket with a lid on top. Bring to the boil, then reduce the heat to low. Add the mushrooms to the steamer, cover and steam for 2 minutes, or until the mushrooms are cooked. Remove from the steamer and keep warm.

Pour the dressing into a small saucepan and bring to a simmer over medium heat.

To serve, arrange the mushrooms and daikon on a platter, place the mackerel on top, pour over the hot dressing, then scatter on the spring onion.

STEAMED FISH WITH TARTARE SAUCE

SERVES 5

barramundi fillets 5 x 160 g, skin on,
pin-boned

+

sea salt and freshly ground black pepper
tartare sauce 90 g (⅓ cup) (page 244)
lemon wedges to serve

This book is all about simplicity and there is nothing simpler than steaming some beautiful pieces of fish and popping them on the dinner table for people to help themselves. I have chosen barramundi as I find it very forgiving when steaming. You need to cook it all the way through, otherwise it will be too tough to be enjoyable. You could also steam salmon, trout, snapper or pretty much any fish you like. This is delicious with your favourite salad or side.

Season the barramundi with salt and pepper.

Line a steamer basket with baking paper. Fill a saucepan with water, bring to the boil, then reduce the heat to low. Place the barramundi in the steamer and set over the pan of simmering water. Cover and steam for 7–8 minutes until the fish is cooked through. Transfer to a plate and allow to rest for 2 minutes, keeping warm.

Serve the barramundi with the tartare sauce and the lemon wedges on the side.

CRISPY SKIN SALMON WITH AVOCADO PUREE AND NORI PASTE

I created this dish as I really wanted to nail a nori paste that I could use to get more iodine and sea vegetables into my diet. I think you are going to love this recipe, which combines the nori paste with ingredients you might traditionally find in a sushi roll, such as salmon, avocado and cucumber.

Preheat the oven to 200°C (180°C fan-forced).

Heat a large ovenproof frying pan over high heat until very hot. Brush the fish with the coconut oil or fat, season with salt and pepper and cook, skin-side down, for 30–60 seconds. Transfer the pan to the oven and cook, still skin-side down, for 3½–4 minutes until medium–rare and the skin is golden and crisp. Flip the salmon and allow it to rest, skin-side up, on a plate for 2–3 minutes, keeping warm. At this point the salmon will be perfectly cooked; moist and a slightly deeper pink in the middle.

Combine the cucumber spirals, a squeeze of lemon juice from one of the wedges and 1 tablespoon of olive oil in a bowl and toss until the cucumber is coated with the dressing.

To serve, smear 1 tablespoon of nori paste onto each serving plate, then dollop on some avocado puree and top with the cucumber spirals and baby shiso leaves (if using). Add a salmon fillet and finish with a drizzle of olive oil, some cracked black pepper and lemon wedges.

SERVES 4

salmon fillets 4 x 160 g, skin on, pin-boned
lebanese cucumbers 4, spiralised
lemon 1, cut into wedges

+

coconut oil or good-quality animal fat
  2 tablespoons, melted
sea salt and freshly ground black pepper
olive oil for drizzling
nori paste 80 g (page 239)
avocado puree 350 g (page 228)
baby shiso leaves to serve (optional)

PRAWN SALAD AND AVOCADO ON TOAST

If you want to lift your avocado on toast game, add some fine-quality seafood to the mix in the way of prawns, crab, smoked fish, lobster or even raw tuna, if that rocks your world. Enjoy this any time of the day or night. I use grain-free and gluten-free paleo bread, but feel free to use any bread or seed crackers you love.

Place the prawns in a bowl, add the herbs, watercress and finger lime and drizzle on a little olive oil. Toss to coat and season with salt and pepper.

To serve, spread the avocado puree on the toast, top with the prawn salad and serve.

SERVES 4

cooked king prawns 16, deveined
  and chopped
**mixed herb leaves (such as mint, dill
  and basil)** 1 handful
watercress sprigs 1 handful
finger limes 2, halved and flesh squeezed out
paleo bread 8 slices, toasted
+
extra-virgin olive oil for drizzling
sea salt and freshly ground black pepper
avocado puree 350 g (page 228)

WHOLE ROASTED FLATHEAD

SERVES 2–4

leeks 2, white part only, thickly sliced
whole flatheads 2 x 900 g, cleaned, scaled
   and gutted (ask your fishmonger to
   do this)
chicken bone broth 500 ml (2 cups)
   (page 231) (or use fish bone broth
   or water)
chervil leaves 1 handful
+
melted coconut oil or good-quality
   animal fat 80 ml (⅓ cup)
fish seasoning 1 tablespoon, plus extra
   if desired (page 219)
freshly ground black pepper
mayonnaise 3 tablespoons (page 237)

This is another favourite of mine in this book, as it is just so real and healthy. A fish cooked whole is an absolute treat because you get to appreciate all the parts, including the cheeks, belly, wings and tail. I have added some delicious leeks cooked in broth to really amp up the flavour profile. If you've never tried leek cooked in broth, please give it a go – it is sensational.

Preheat the oven to 200°C (180°C fan-forced).

Arrange the leek in a single layer in a large roasting tin.

Using a sharp knife, score the fish by making small incisions into the flesh on both sides.

Rub the coconut oil or fat into the fish and season generously with the fish seasoning and pepper. Transfer the fish to the roasting tin and pour in the broth. Roast for 20–35 minutes until the fish is golden and cooked through and the leek is tender.

To serve, place the fish on large serving plates and add the leek. Dollop on some mayonnaise, scatter over the chervil and sprinkle with pepper and a little more fish seasoning, if desired.

SARDINES WITH FENNEL AND CURRANTS

Sardines are so delicious, yet I feel people steer clear of them as they have not had a chance to really appreciate them. One of the best ways to enjoy sardines is whole (head, bones and all). However, if you are a bit squeamish, I suggest you try them filleted and butterflied, then simply pan-fry and serve them with an acidic dressing. And that should make the fussiest of eaters happy. The aniseed flavour and freshness of the fennel and currant salad rounds this dish off perfectly.

SERVES 4

fennel bulb 1 large, finely shaved, fronds reserved
currants 3 tablespoons
sardine fillets 12, butterflied
+
french dressing 100 ml (page 233), plus extra to serve (optional)
sea salt and freshly ground black pepper
coconut oil or good-quality animal fat 2 tablespoons

Place the shaved fennel, fennel fronds and currants in a bowl, add the dressing and toss to coat. Season with salt and pepper if needed.

Season the sardine fillets with salt and pepper.

Heat the coconut oil or fat in a large frying pan over medium–high heat, add the sardines, skin-side down, in batches and cook for 40 seconds, or until crisp and golden. Turn and cook for 10 seconds, or until just cooked through.

Place the sardines on a platter or serving plates, arrange the salad on the side and drizzle over some more dressing, if desired. Serve.

WHOLE BAKED WHITING WITH ASPARAGUS

SERVES 2

whole whiting 2 x 300–350 g, cleaned,
scaled and gutted (ask your fishmonger
to do this)
asparagus 3 bunches (about 400 g),
woody ends trimmed
garlic cloves 4, finely sliced
finely chopped flat-leaf parsley leaves
2 tablespoons
lemons 2
+
coconut oil or good-quality animal fat
3 tablespoons, melted
sea salt and freshly ground black pepper
extra-virgin olive oil 2 tablespoons

I used to fish with my good mate Udo at Bondi quite a lot when I lived there. We would snorkel to find the whiting, then run back up the rocks, pop a worm on a hook and cast out to where we could see the school. Usually, a minute or two later, we would have a bite on the end of our lines. The beautiful thing about living so close to the beach is, after catching and cleaning the fish, it takes less than an hour to whip up a simple dish like this and pop it on the table. This is fast food at its best.

Preheat the oven to 220°C (200°C fan-forced). Line a baking tray with baking paper.

Place the whiting on the prepared tray, drizzle on 1 tablespoon of the coconut oil or fat and rub it in all over to coat evenly. Season with salt and pepper. Roast for 10–14 minutes until just cooked through. Transfer to a plate and allow to rest for a few minutes, keeping warm.

Meanwhile, heat the remaining coconut oil or fat in a large frying pan over medium–high heat. Add the asparagus and sauté for 3 minutes, then add the garlic and parsley and continue to cook, tossing frequently, for 2 minutes, or until the garlic is golden and the asparagus is just tender. Remove from the heat, drizzle on the olive oil and squeeze half a lemon over, then gently toss. Season to taste with salt and pepper.

Arrange the asparagus and fish on the baking tray or a large platter. Spoon the remaining garlic dressing in the pan over the fish and asparagus. Cut the remaining lemon into cheeks and serve on the side.

TROUT WITH PISTACHIO GREMOLATA AND PICKLED ONION

I cooked this dish using local trout for a special dinner at the Thredbo snowfields last year. It was a winner, and everyone loved it. Why not give it a whirl if you have family coming over for a celebration, as it is super easy and super yummy.

Season the trout fillets with salt and pepper.

Heat the coconut oil or fat in a large frying pan over high heat. Add the trout fillets, skin-side down, and fry for 1 ½ minutes, then flip and cook for 15–20 seconds until the fish is just cooked through. Transfer to a plate and allow to rest for 2 minutes, keeping warm.

Place the trout on a platter, spoon on the gremolata, scatter over the pickled onion and pistachios and serve with the lemon wedges on the side.

SERVES 4

trout fillets 4 x 140–160 g, skin on, pin-boned
pistachio kernels 2 tablespoons, finely chopped
+
sea salt and freshly ground black pepper
coconut oil or good-quality animal fat 2 tablespoons
pistachio gremolata 100 g (page 240)
pickled red onion 200 g (page 240)
lemon wedges to serve

CHICKEN & DUCK

ROAST CHICKEN LEGS WITH SILVERBEET AND GARLIC

A classic roast chicken has always been a favourite of mine and it has become a firm favourite for my kids, too. Roast garlic is a chook's best friend and should always be added to the roasting tin. My daughters will each polish off a whole bulb of roast garlic ... not a clove, a whole bulb! It's just that delicious. Serve the chicken with any veg you love. At our place we like to throw some greens into the roasting tin once the chicken comes out, so they soak up all the yummy juices.

Preheat the oven to 180°C (160°C fan-forced).

Rub 1 tablespoon of the coconut oil or fat into the chicken and sprinkle over the chicken seasoning and a little pepper. Place in a large, shallow bowl, cover and allow to marinate in the fridge for 15 minutes.

Place the chicken, skin-side up, in a roasting tin. Add the garlic bulbs, cut-side down, and roast for 40 minutes, or until the chicken is golden and the juices run clear when the thigh is pierced with a skewer. Transfer to a plate and allow to rest for a few minutes, keeping warm.

Meanwhile, heat the remaining coconut oil or fat in a frying pan over medium heat. Add the silverbeet leaves and 3 tablespoons of water and cook for 4 minutes, or until the stems are almost tender. Season with salt and pepper.

Divide the silverbeet among warm serving plates, add the chicken and garlic and serve with the dressing on the side to pour over the chicken and silverbeet.

SERVES 4

chicken marylands 4
garlic bulbs 2, halved horizontally
silverbeet ½ bunch (about 6 leaves), trimmed

+

coconut oil or good-quality animal fat
   3 tablespoons, melted
chicken seasoning 3 teaspoons (page 218)
sea salt and freshly ground black pepper
french dressing 200 ml (page 232)

CHICKEN MEATBALLS WITH EGG YOLK SAUCE

SERVES 2

chicken mince 400 g
spring onions 2, white and green parts
    separated, whites finely sliced and
    greens shredded
ginger 2 cm piece, finely grated
tamari 3 teaspoons
egg yolks 2
+
melted coconut oil or good-quality
    animal fat 1 tablespoon
japanese dressing 80 ml (⅓ cup) (page 236)

On a recent family skiing trip to Japan, we had the good fortune to explore different cities and their unique styles of Japanese food. One dish I particularly loved was *tsukune*, which is basically a chicken meatball served with an egg yolk and soy sauce. Generally, when this is made in Japan, they use lots of skin and other parts of the chicken, making the meatballs a chicken-flavoured powerhouse; for ease here I have used chicken mince.

Soak seven bamboo skewers in cold water for 20 minutes (or use metal skewers). Drain.

Preheat the oven to 200°C (180°C fan-forced) and line a baking tray with baking paper.

Place the chicken, spring onion whites, ginger, tamari and coconut oil or fat in a large bowl and mix to combine. Roll into 14 small balls about 4 cm in diameter. Thread two balls onto each skewer.

Place the skewers on the prepared tray and bake for 10–12 minutes, or until cooked through.

Meanwhile, to make a dipping sauce, place the egg yolks and dressing in a small serving bowl and swirl to combine.

Arrange the skewers on a platter, scatter over the spring onion greens and serve with the dipping sauce.

CONFIT DUCK LEGS

MAKES 4

duck legs 4
garlic 1 head, cloves separated
thyme sprigs small handful
+
sea salt 2 ½ tablespoons
melted duck or goose fat, coconut oil
    or olive oil 800 ml

If there is one dish in the world that I think everyone should try at least once, it has to be the French classic *confit de canard* – or confit duck to you and me. The first time I tried it I was speechless, seriously. I had never tasted anything so indulgently luxurious. The duck legs are slowly cooked in their own fat until they are fork tender and just falling off the bone. To add to this, they are sometimes roasted so they are crispy skinned and the flavour develops even further. I would have to say this is in my top ten recipes of all time.

Rub the salt into the duck legs to evenly coat. Cover and refrigerate for 12 hours or, for best results, 24 hours. Turn the legs from time to time.

Preheat the oven to 130°C (110°C fan-forced).

Pat the duck legs dry with paper towel. Do not rub or wash off the salt. Place the duck legs in a single layer in a large casserole dish and add the garlic and thyme. Pour over the fat or oil to completely submerge the duck legs, cover with the lid and roast for 2 ½ hours, or until the duck is very tender.

Remove the duck legs from the fat or oil and carefully pat dry with paper towel. (Reserve the fat or oil to use in other dishes.)

Increase the oven temperature to 200°C (180°C fan-forced).

Place the duck legs on a tray and bake for 15 minutes, skin-side up, until golden brown. Eat at once. Alternatively, allow the duck legs to cool completely at room temperature in the fat, then transfer the legs and fat to an airtight storage container and refrigerate. Store in the fridge for up to 1 week or in the freezer for up to 3 months.

Tip: I often use half duck fat and half coconut oil for making confit dishes at home, which always produces a great result.

JOY'S YUMMY CHINESE CHICKEN

SERVES 4

chicken drumsticks 1.2 kg
lemon 1, cut into wedges
garlic bulbs 2, halved horizontally
spring onions 3, cut into matchsticks
+
tamari and ginger marinade 200 ml
   (page 243)
coriander leaves to serve
sesame seeds to serve

Growing up, Mum used to make the most amazing Chinese-inspired chicken wings with soy sauce, lemon and garlic. For this book I wanted to recreate something similar that could be served as a main meal, so instead I've used chicken legs. They still have the same delicious flavour – just a bit meatier. You can easily make this dish with little fuss for a large family or for a celebration. Serve with some bok choy or a simple Asian salad.

Place half the marinade in a large, shallow bowl. Add the chicken legs and turn to coat. Cover and refrigerate for at least 1 hour, or ideally overnight.

Preheat the oven to 200°C (180°C fan-forced).

Transfer the chicken legs and marinade to a large roasting tin, spread out in a single layer and add the lemon wedges and garlic. Roast, turning the legs occasionally, for 40–45 minutes until they are golden and the juices run clear when the thickest part of the leg is pierced with a skewer. Transfer to a plate and allow to rest for a few minutes, keeping warm.

Place the remaining marinade in a saucepan over medium heat and bring to a simmer.

Arrange the chicken legs on a platter, spoon over the hot marinade and top with the spring onion. Sprinkle with the coriander and sesame seeds and serve.

CHICKEN AND GARLIC BROTH

SERVES 4–6

chicken bone broth 1.6 litres (page 231)
boneless chicken thighs 600 g, skin on
   or off
garlic cloves 8, finely sliced
+
sea salt and freshly ground black pepper

When you are sick there isn't much that beats a bowl of steaming chicken soup. The aroma from a big batch of chicken broth is one of the most delicious smells to come out of the kitchen. I have kept this recipe super, super simple with the addition of healing garlic.

Place the chicken broth, chicken and garlic in a large saucepan over medium heat and bring to a simmer. Reduce the heat to medium–low and gently simmer for 40 minutes, or until the chicken is cooked through and tender.

Remove the chicken from the broth, shred, then add back to the broth. Season with salt and pepper, ladle into bowls and serve.

Tip: Try adding some sliced fresh ginger or healing spice blend (page 220) to this dish for an extra health boost.

PETE'S PEKING DUCK

SERVES 4

duck breasts 4 x 180 g, skin on

baby cos lettuces 2, leaves separated

spring onions 2, cut into 7 cm strips,
   plus extra, sliced, to serve

lebanese cucumber 1, halved lengthways,
   deseeded and cut into 7 cm strips

+

sea salt

coconut oil or good-quality animal fat
   2 teaspoons

hoisin sauce 200 ml (page 234)

black and white sesame seeds, toasted,
   to serve

For about 20 years I did outside catering and loved the adrenaline of setting up an instant kitchen on site somewhere for a birthday party, anniversary, wedding or product launch. One of the most-loved dishes we served was Peking duck pancakes. Over time I adapted the traditional wraps and swapped them out for lettuce leaves – and people enjoy them just as much, if not more. The paleo hoisin recipe is so easy and yummy, you'll want to use it a lot.

Preheat the oven to 180°C (160°C fan-forced).

Season the duck skin with salt.

Heat the coconut oil or fat in an ovenproof frying pan over medium heat. Add the duck breasts, skin-side down, and fry for 7–8 minutes until well browned. Turn the duck breasts, skin-side up, and transfer to the oven to roast for 5–6 minutes for medium–rare. If you prefer your duck to be well done, roast for a couple more minutes. Place on a plate and allow to rest for 5 minutes, keeping warm.

Slice the duck and arrange on the lettuce leaves, then drizzle over the hoisin sauce and top with the spring onion and cucumber strips. Scatter on the sesame seeds and the extra sliced spring onion and serve.

TURMERIC AND LEMONGRASS CHICKEN SKEWERS

SERVES 4

boneless chicken thighs 4, skin on, halved
lemongrass 4 stems
+
turmeric spice rub 200 g (page 224)
sea salt and freshly ground black pepper
coconut oil or good-quality animal fat
   3 tablespoons, melted

Cucumber and mint salad

lebanese cucumbers 2, halved lengthways
   and thickly sliced on the diagonal
mint leaves 1 large handful, torn or
   roughly chopped
thai dressing 80 ml (⅓ cup) (page 244)
sea salt and freshly ground black pepper
   if needed

These tasty morsels are perfect for a weeknight dinner. And on the weekend, when friends and family pop in, any barbecue would welcome their addition, as they are easy to make and look amazing. I love to serve a simple and refreshing salad alongside – you don't really need much more to make a meal that everyone will love.

Place the turmeric spice rub in a shallow bowl. Add the chicken and toss until thoroughly coated. Cover and place in the fridge to marinate for at least 30 minutes, but ideally 2 hours.

To make the skewers, peel off the outer leaves on the lemongrass stems to reveal the pale part, then cut the stems into eight 12 cm lengths.

Thread the marinated chicken onto the lemongrass skewers and season with salt and pepper.

Heat a barbecue grill plate to medium or a chargrill pan over medium heat. Brush with the coconut oil or fat, add the skewers and cook, turning occasionally and basting with extra marinade from the bowl, for 10–12 minutes, or until the chicken is cooked through. Transfer to a plate and allow to rest for 5 minutes, keeping warm.

Meanwhile, to make the salad, place the cucumber and mint in a bowl, add the dressing and toss to coat. Season with salt and pepper if needed.

Arrange the skewers on a platter and serve with the cucumber and mint salad on the side.

SPICED CHICKEN WITH PICKLED RED ONION SALAD

Chicken is one of the most popular meats eaten at dinner tables in Australia, and often features at least once a week. So, I've made it my mission to find exciting ways to deliver delicious chicken recipes to you. This salad ticks all the boxes when it comes to ease of preparation, taste and being a fun dish to serve to family and friends.

Preheat the oven to 200°C (180°C fan-forced).

Pat the chicken dry with paper towel. Cover the entire bird with the coconut oil or fat and rub in the spice blend to evenly coat the skin.

Brush a chargrill pan with a little oil and place over high heat. Add the chicken and cook on both sides for 2–3 minutes, or until nicely charred.

Place the chicken in a roasting tin and roast, basting occasionally with the juices in the tin, for 40–45 minutes until golden and the juices run clear when the thigh is pierced with a skewer. Transfer to a plate and allow to rest for 5 minutes, keeping warm. Cut the chicken into eight portions.

Just before you are ready to serve, place the parsley and pickled red onion in a bowl, pour over half the dressing, then toss to coat. Season with salt and pepper.

Arrange the chicken and salad on a large platter, drizzle over a little more dressing and serve with the remaining dressing on the side.

SERVES 4

chicken 1 x 1.8 kg, butterflied
flat-leaf parsley leaves 2 large handfuls
+
coconut oil or good-quality animal fat 3 tablespoons, plus extra oil for brushing
coriander and cumin spice blend 2 ½ tablespoons (page 219)
pickled red onion 150 g (page 240)
middle eastern dressing 80 ml (⅓ cup) (page 238)
sea salt and freshly ground black pepper

VIETNAMESE-STYLE CHICKEN LIVERS WITH BEAN SPROUTS AND HERBS

One of the greatest joys in life has to be the experience of eating and learning about different cuisines and ingredients. Recently, I went to the Melbourne restaurant Anchovy, which serves modern Vietnamese cuisine, and they had chicken livers on the menu. Of course, I had to order them – and they were sublime. I have tried to recreate the dish here as best as I can and, I gotta say, it is one of my new favourite ways to eat chicken livers. I hope you enjoy.

Rinse the chicken livers under cold water, pat dry with paper towel and trim off any fat, sinew and veins. Set aside.

Heat the coconut oil or fat in a large frying pan over medium–high heat. Add the chicken livers in batches (taking care as the oil may spit) and cook, turning frequently, for 3 ½–4 minutes until slightly pink in the middle or cooked to your liking. Season with salt and transfer to a bowl.

Add the mint, then the dressing to the chicken livers and toss to coat.

Arrange the chicken livers on serving plates, top with the bean sprouts and drizzle with olive oil.

SERVES 4

chicken livers 700 g
vietnamese mint leaves 2 large handfuls
bean sprouts 2 large handfuls, trimmed
+
coconut oil or good-quality animal fat
    2 tablespoons
sea salt
thai dressing 140 ml (page 244)
extra-virgin olive oil for drizzling

CRACKLING BARBECUE CHICKEN

I think we can all remember the first time we tried a barbecue spice blend. It might have been on a takeaway chicken or some deep-fried chips, or maybe even a handful of biscuits from a box of Shapes. Well, the classics never disappear; they provide so much joy for our tastebuds and that is reason enough for us to keep them in our cooking repertoire. Here, we have the ultimate barbecue taste sensation: juicy chicken thighs with barbecue seasoning cooked until the skin is golden and crackling.

SERVES 4

boneless chicken thighs 8, skin on
mixed salad leaves 2 handfuls

+

sea salt 2 teaspoons
coconut oil or good-quality animal fat
  2 teaspoons
barbecue spice blend 1 teaspoon (page 218),
  plus extra to serve
lemon wedges to serve

Flatten the chicken thighs to an even thickness with a mallet. Season the skin with salt.

Heat the coconut oil or fat in a large, heavy-based frying pan over medium–high heat. Add four of the thighs, skin-side down, and sprinkle over ½ teaspoon of the barbecue spice blend. Fry the chicken, undisturbed, for 6–8 minutes until the skin is crispy and golden brown. Flip and cook for 3 minutes, or until cooked through. Transfer to a plate, keeping warm. Repeat with the remaining chicken.

Sprinkle the remaining barbecue spice blend over the crispy chicken skin and serve with the salad leaves and lemon wedges.

ROAST CONFIT DUCK WITH BRAISED CABBAGE AND OLIVES

SERVES 4

red cabbage ½, cut into 2 cm thick slices
confit duck legs 4 (page 104)
pitted kalamata olives 100 g (⅔ cup), halved
+
**confit fat (from the confit duck legs) or
    good-quality animal fat** 3 tablespoons
sea salt and freshly ground black pepper
jus 150 ml (page 237)
micro herbs to serve (optional)

Confit duck is my daughter Indii's favourite meal. She can eat two whole legs in one sitting, which is pretty impressive for a 13 year old. I am rapt every time she asks for more as I know she is getting good animal fats and proteins into her body. You can serve confit duck with anything you like, but the classic pairing with cabbage is one of my favourites.

Preheat the oven to 180°C (160°C fan-forced).

Place the cabbage in a roasting tin, drizzle over 2 tablespoons of fat and season with salt and pepper. Pour over 250 ml (1 cup) of water, cover with baking paper and roast for 1 hour, or until the cabbage is tender. Set aside, keeping warm.

Increase the oven temperature to 220°C (200°C fan-forced). Lightly grease a roasting tin with the remaining fat.

Pat the duck legs dry with paper towel, being careful not to break the skin. Arrange the duck legs in a single layer in the prepared tin and roast for 15–20 minutes until golden. Sprinkle with a little salt, if needed.

Pour the jus into a small saucepan, place over medium–low heat and bring to a simmer.

To serve, arrange the cabbage on plates. Top with a roast duck leg, drizzle over the jus and finish with the olives and micro herbs (if using).

ROAST CHICKEN WITH MUSHROOMS

SERVES 4

chicken marylands 4
enoki mushrooms 300 g, trimmed
lemon ½
+
sea salt and freshly ground black pepper
coconut oil or good-quality animal fat
   3 tablespoons
chinese dressing 275 ml (page 232)
extra-virgin olive oil for drizzling

I'm always looking for new ways to prepare chicken to entice not only my own family but also you, my readers. The goal is to keep it simple and let the natural flavours of the chicken shine. In my kitchen I use organic chicken and I encourage you to use the best you can source. I often have chicken legs in the freezer, as I feel they are the tastiest part of the chicken (except for the liver, of course!). Here, I serve the chicken with enoki mushrooms and a delicious Chinese dressing.

Preheat the oven to 180°C (160°C fan-forced).

Season the chicken with salt.

Heat 2 tablespoons of the coconut oil or fat in a large heavy-based roasting tin over medium–high heat. Add the chicken, skin-side down, and cook for 2–3 minutes, then turn and cook for a further 2 minutes, or until browned on each side. Place in the oven and roast for 45 minutes, or until the chicken is golden and the juices run clear when the thigh is pierced with a skewer. Transfer the chicken to a plate and allow to rest for a few minutes, keeping warm.

Meanwhile, heat the remaining oil or fat in the roasting tin over medium heat. Add the enoki mushrooms and sauté for 1½–2 minutes, or until tender. Season with a little salt and pepper.

To serve, divide the mushrooms among serving plates, add the chicken and pour over the Chinese dressing. Finish with a squeeze of lemon juice and a drizzle of olive oil.

ROASTED LEMON AND GARLIC CHICKEN

SERVES 4

chicken 1 x 1.8 kg
garlic bulbs 2, halved horizontally or
   cloves separated
lemon 1, sliced, plus extra wedges to serve
french shallots 8, peeled
+
coconut oil or good-quality animal fat
   3 tablespoons, melted
sea salt and freshly ground black pepper
chicken bone broth 400 ml (page 231)
flat-leaf parsley leaves finely chopped,
   to serve (optional)

This classic French dish of roast chicken with lemon, shallots and garlic is, in my mind, a perfect meal. The combination of the acidity from the lemon, mixed with the garlicky chicken juices and roasted shallots really is sensational. Plus the whole thing is made in one dish!

Preheat the oven to 200°C (180°C fan-forced).

Rinse the chicken inside and out, pat dry with paper towel, then rub on the coconut oil or fat and season generously inside and out with salt and pepper. Tie the legs up with kitchen string.

Place the chicken in a casserole dish, scatter around the garlic, lemon slices and shallots and pour in the broth. Roast, basting occasionally with the juices in the dish, for 40 minutes. Reduce the temperature to 170°C (150°C fan-forced) and roast for a further 30–45 minutes until the chicken is golden and the juices run clear when the thigh is pierced with a skewer. Allow the chicken to rest for 10 minutes before sprinkling on the parsley, if using, and serving with the lemon wedges.

MEAT

BLT WEDGES

SERVES 4–6

rindless bacon 4 rashers
iceberg lettuce 1, cored and cut into
   6 wedges
roma tomatoes 3, cut into 3 cm chunks
flat-leaf parsley leaves 1 small handful,
   roughly chopped
+
coconut oil or good-quality animal fat
   1 teaspoon
sea salt and freshly ground black pepper
caesar dressing or mayonnaise 100 g
   (page 230 or 237)
extra-virgin olive oil for drizzling

Bacon, lettuce and tomato work so well as a salad. You have the freshness and crunch of the lettuce (especially if it has just come out of the fridge), the sweet juiciness and acidity of ripe tomatoes and, finally, the fatty and crispy bacon to bring everything together. A simple dressing or mayo-based sauce is all you need to finish it off. If you want to make this dish more substantial, try adding some sliced steak, boiled eggs or smoked fish.

Heat the coconut oil or fat in a frying pan over medium heat. Add the bacon and cook on both sides for 5–8 minutes until golden and crisp. Roughly chop the bacon and set aside, keeping warm.

Place the iceberg wedges on a platter, then scatter over the tomato and bacon. Season with salt and pepper. Pour on the dressing or mayonnaise, sprinkle over the parsley and finish with a drizzle of olive oil.

PEPPER STEAK

SERVES 4

eye fillet steaks 4 x 180 g, at room
  temperature
+
coconut oil or good-quality animal fat
  2 tablespoons, melted
sea salt
coarsely ground black pepper 1 tablespoon
jus 200 ml (page 237)
your choice of greens or side to serve
dijon mustard to serve

There's a reason why chefs season a lot with salt and pepper and, really, it's very simple. These kitchen staples elevate the flavour to let the ingredients shine. To highlight the power of these super spices, I just had to include a pepper steak recipe. Now, you may think there is a lot of pepper used here – and there is! That's because the eye fillet needs more help than some of the fattier steak cuts to make it taste sensational.

Heat a barbecue grill plate to hot or a large chargrill pan over high heat.

Brush the steaks with the coconut oil or fat, season with a good pinch of salt and sprinkle over the pepper. Cook the steaks on one side for 2–3 minutes, then flip and cook for a further 2–3 minutes for medium–rare (or cook to your liking). Transfer the steaks to a plate and allow to rest for 4–6 minutes, keeping warm.

Meanwhile, pour the jus into a saucepan and bring to a simmer over medium heat.

Serve the steaks with the warm jus, your choice of greens or side and some mustard.

Tip: Keep the pepper a bit chunky for extra texture and flavour.

PORK SAUSAGES WITH POACHED EGGS AND ROMESCO SAUCE

SERVES 4

paleo pork sausages 8, at room temperature
white vinegar or apple cider vinegar
   80 ml (⅓ cup)
eggs 8
red vein sorrel or rocket leaves
   1 large handful
+
coconut oil or good-quality animal fat
   1 tablespoon
romesco sauce 225 g (page 241)
freshly ground black pepper

Sausages and eggs make the best quick meal. Some people love to keep theirs super simple with a tomato or barbecue sauce; however, a wonderfully rich Spanish romesco sauce – made from roasted capsicums and almonds – is truly something special. Once you have a batch on hand, you can use it for so many different dishes, as it pairs beautifully with seafood, vegetables and all types of meat. I cook this dish often for myself and my family.

Heat the coconut oil or fat in a large frying pan over medium heat. Add the sausages and cook until browned on all sides and just cooked through, about 8 minutes. Set aside, keeping warm.

Meanwhile, pour the vinegar into a saucepan of boiling salted water, then reduce the heat to medium–low so the water is just simmering. Crack an egg into a cup. Using a wooden spoon, stir the simmering water in one direction to form a whirlpool and drop the egg into the centre. Repeat with the remaining eggs and cook for 3 minutes, or until the eggs are poached to your liking. Remove the eggs with a slotted spoon and place on paper towel to drain.

Spoon 2 tablespoons of romesco sauce onto each plate, then top with two poached eggs and two sausages. Finish with the sorrel or rocket and a good grind of pepper.

STEAK AND CHIPS

SERVES 4

sirloin steaks 4 x 200 g, at room temperature
mixed salad leaves 2 large handfuls
salad dressing of your choice 3 tablespoons
sweet potato fries (page 200)

+

coconut oil or good-quality animal fat
   2 tablespoons, melted
sea salt and freshly ground black pepper
mayonnaise 80 g (⅓ cup) (page 237)

It's strange how some much-loved foods from only a generation ago are not as popular as they once were. Take, for instance, steak and chips. It was one of the most popular dishes in Australia – at home and in restaurants – and was served up for breakfast, lunch and dinner. Now, you often have to go to a good steak restaurant to find it. And that is why I wanted to include this dish, as I believe it deserves to be on our tables more often. My only tweak? I swapped the potato chips for sweet potato fries.

Heat a barbecue hotplate to hot or a large frying pan over high heat.

Brush the steaks with a little coconut oil or fat and season with salt and pepper. Cook the steaks on one side for 2–3 minutes, then flip and cook for a further 2–3 minutes for medium–rare (or cook to your liking). Transfer to a plate and allow to rest for 4–6 minutes, keeping warm.

Place the salad leaves in a bowl and dress with the dressing. Season with salt and pepper.

Place the steaks on serving plates, arrange the sweet potato fries and salad on the side and serve with a dollop of mayonnaise.

Tip: I like to add a fried egg to this dish.

LAMB CHOPS WITH WATERCRESS AND FENNEL SALAD

SERVES 2–4

lamb forequarter chops 4
+
greek seasoning 2 teaspoons (page 220)
coconut oil or good-quality animal fat
2 tablespoons

Watercress and fennel salad
watercress sprigs 2 large handfuls
fennel bulb ½, finely sliced, fronds reserved
finely chopped preserved lemon rind
1 tablespoon
lemon juice 2 tablespoons
extra-virgin olive oil 3 tablespoons
sea salt and freshly ground black pepper

Humble lamb chops featured on the dinner table quite frequently in my younger years; so, nowadays, I feel nostalgic whenever I cook and eat them. In an effort to keep things simple, the lamb – the star of this dish – is complemented by the classic Greek flavours of oregano, lemon and garlic. If you, like me, eat your chops with your hands, you will have the most joy licking your fingers between each bite of lamb. A dressed salad on the side is all you need to complete this dish.

Season the lamb chops generously with the Greek seasoning.

Heat the coconut oil or fat in a large frying pan over medium–high heat. Add the lamb chops and cook, turning occasionally, for 6–7 minutes for medium–rare (or cook to your liking). Transfer to a plate and allow to rest for 5 minutes, keeping warm.

Meanwhile, to make the salad, place the watercress, sliced fennel, fennel fronds and preserved lemon in a bowl. Add the lemon juice and olive oil and gently toss to evenly coat the salad. Season with salt and pepper.

Arrange the salad on serving plates, add the lamb chops and serve.

CRISPY PORK BELLY

The Japanese way of cooking pork belly, which ensures a beautiful crispy crackling, is one to be revered and is well worth attempting at home. I love the simplicity of serving a slab of pork belly this way, as everyone loves going back for more and more. You can pop a salad on the side if you like, such as a slaw, which will round it off nicely.

SERVES 6

boneless pork belly 1.2 kg, skin scored, at room temperature
+
boiling water 250 ml (1 cup)
coconut oil or good-quality animal fat 2 tablespoons
sea salt
japanese spice blend 1–2 teaspoons (page 221)
japanese dressing 140 ml (page 236)
hot english or dijon mustard to serve

Preheat the oven to 240°C (220°C fan-forced) – you need to start by blasting the pork with heat.

Place the pork on a wire rack in the kitchen sink, carefully pour the boiling water over the skin, then pat dry with paper towel.

Rub the coconut oil or fat into the pork skin, season with a good amount of salt and place the pork in a large, deep roasting tin. Roast for 35–40 minutes until the skin starts to bubble. Reduce the temperature to 150°C (130°C fan-forced) and continue to roast the pork for 1¼ hours, or until the flesh is very tender. Transfer to a plate and allow to rest for 15 minutes, keeping warm. If the crackling isn't crisp enough, place the pork, crackling-side up, under a hot grill for a few minutes.

Cut the pork into bite-sized pieces and arrange on a platter, sprinkle over the Japanese spice blend and serve with the Japanese dressing and mustard on the side for dipping.

SIMPLE SCOTCH FILLET WITH STONE FRUIT

The addition of grilled stone fruit to a steak dish might sound a little strange – I certainly thought so before I tried it, but then I absolutely loved it. I guess you could call this a salad if you like, and serve it either warm or cold. It would make for a perfect work or school lunch the next day.

Heat a barbecue grill plate and hotplate to hot or a chargrill pan and large frying pan over high heat.

Brush the nectarine with 1 tablespoon of the coconut oil or fat, then chargrill for 3 minutes on each side until softened and charred. Set aside.

SERVES 4

nectarines 4, cut into cheeks and wedges
scotch fillet steaks 4 x 180 g, at room
   temperature
baby rocket leaves 2 large handfuls
+
coconut oil or good-quality animal fat
   2 tablespoons, melted
sea salt and freshly ground black pepper
italian dressing 3 tablespoons (page 235)

Brush the steaks with the remaining coconut oil or fat and season with a generous amount of salt and pepper. Cook the steaks on the hotplate or in the frying pan for 2–2 ½ minutes on each side for medium–rare (or cook to your liking). Transfer to a plate and allow to rest for 4 minutes, keeping warm.

Meanwhile, place the rocket and nectarine in a bowl, add the dressing and gently toss. Season with salt and pepper.

To serve, thickly slice the steak and arrange on serving plates with the salad.

SAUSAGE SANGA

SERVES 4

onion 1, sliced
paleo sausages of your choice 4
paleo bread 4 slices
+
coconut oil or good-quality animal fat
   2 tablespoons
sea salt and freshly ground black pepper
tomato ketchup 80 g (¼ cup) (page 245)

We can thank Bunnings and Surf Life Saving Australia for turning the humble sausage sanga into a national icon. I am a fan, I have to say, and have eaten my fair share of sausages in white bread with the obligatory sugar-filled tomato sauce over the years. However, there are healthier alternatives that are just as delicious. Here, we serve some beautiful paleo sausages with paleo bread and paleo tomato sauce … did I mention it was paleo? It's only a matter of time till Bunnings and Surf Life Saving Australia add this as an option.

Melt 1 tablespoon of the coconut oil or fat in a non-stick frying pan over medium heat. Add the onion and sauté for 8 minutes, or until softened and starting to caramelise. Season with salt and pepper, then remove from the pan and set aside, keeping warm.

Wipe the pan clean, add the remaining coconut oil or fat and place over medium–high heat. Add the sausages, reduce the heat to medium and cook, turning occasionally, for 8–10 minutes until just cooked through. Season with salt and pepper.

Place the slices of bread on serving plates. Top each slice with a sausage and some onion, dollop on a spoonful of tomato ketchup and serve.

INDIAN-SPICED ROAST BEEF

SERVES 4

beef tri-tip roast 700 g

+

coconut oil or good-quality animal fat
2 tablespoons, melted

indian spice blend 1 tablespoon (page 221)

mint sauce 250 ml (page 238)

lemon wedges to serve

You will never look at a humble piece of beef in the same way after trying this roast enhanced with Indian flavours. The sheer freshness of the mint sauce combined with the fragrant spiced beef will have you coming back for more ... and more. This dish is also great eaten cold the next day for a work or school lunch.

Place the beef on a tray, drizzle over the coconut oil or fat and turn to coat. Sprinkle over the spice blend and massage into the beef, ensuring it is well coated. Cover and refrigerate for 2 hours or, for best results, overnight.

Remove the beef from the fridge 30–40 minutes before you want to cook it to allow it to come to room temperature.

Preheat the oven to 210°C (190°C fan-forced).

Place the beef in a roasting tin and roast for 40 minutes for medium–rare (55–60°C using a meat thermometer) or for 45 minutes for medium (62–66°C). If you like your meat well done, roast for a further 10 minutes (69–72°C). Cover loosely with foil and rest for 10 minutes before carving.

Slice the beef and arrange on a large platter, then pour over the juices from the tin. Serve with the mint sauce and lemon wedges on the side.

KANGAROO WITH CELERIAC REMOULADE

Kangaroo may not be your first choice when it comes to red meat, but I adore it – and I think you will love it, too. The key thing with roo is to not overcook it; you want it rare to medium–rare. This simple celeriac remoulade adds creaminess and a fresh texture that works a treat with the roo. Oh, and by the way, all the steak recipes in this book can easily be replaced with kangaroo, if you like.

Rub the spice blend over the kangaroo fillets, season with salt and pepper and set aside.

Heat the coconut oil or fat in a large frying pan over medium–high heat. Add the kangaroo in two batches and cook, turning, for 5 ½–6 minutes for medium–rare. Transfer to a plate and allow to rest for 5 minutes, keeping warm.

To make the remoulade, coarsely grate the celeriac into a bowl (or you can julienne it or use a serrated peeler), add the mayonnaise and mix well to combine. Season with salt and pepper.

Thickly slice the kangaroo.

To serve, divide the remoulade among serving plates, scatter over the sorrel or rocket, top with the kangaroo and sprinkle with the extra spice blend. Finish with a drizzle of olive oil.

SERVES 4

kangaroo fillets 4 x 160 g, at room
temperature
red vein sorrel or baby rocket leaves
1 large handful
+
middle eastern spice blend 1 tablespoon,
plus extra to serve (page 222)
sea salt and freshly ground black pepper
coconut oil or good-quality animal fat
2 tablespoons
olive oil for drizzling

Celeriac remoulade
celeriac 1 (about 480 g), peeled
mayonnaise 160 g (page 237)
sea salt and freshly ground black pepper

HOT DOGS

SERVES 4

onion 1 large, sliced
paleo beef hot dogs 4
baby cos lettuce leaves 4
dill pickles 70 g, finely sliced
+
coconut oil or good-quality animal fat
    2 tablespoons, plus extra if needed
sea salt and freshly ground black pepper
tomato ketchup 80 g (¼ cup) (page 245)
american or dijon mustard to serve

Cooking doesn't get much easier – or yummier – than this. My reinvented classic hot dogs can be on the table in less than ten minutes and are an effortless entertaining idea, perfect for when you want something to please the fussiest of kids and the most gourmet of grown-up eaters. Make sure you purchase good-quality hot dogs that are made with only the best ingredients. To serve, simply put everything out on the table and let people create their dog of choice. Other serving options include seaweed sheets, kimchi, spiced mayo and, if you feel like traditional bread rolls, some seed buns.

Melt the coconut oil or fat in a non-stick frying pan over medium heat. Add the onion and sauté for 6 minutes, or until softened and starting to caramelise. Season with salt and pepper, then remove from the pan and set aside, keeping warm.

Heat a barbecue grill plate to medium–hot or a chargrill pan over medium–high heat. Brush with some extra coconut oil or fat if needed, then add the hot dogs and cook for 6–8 minutes until heated through and charred. Set aside, keeping warm. Alternatively, fill a saucepan with water and bring to a gentle simmer (do not boil). Add the hot dogs and cook for 4 minutes, or until heated through. Carefully remove the hot dogs with a slotted spoon or tongs and place on paper towel to drain.

Place a hot dog lengthways in the centre of a lettuce leaf. Scatter over the onion and pickle, then dollop on some ketchup and mustard and serve.

CHILLI'S STEAK AND EGG ON PUMPKIN 'TOAST'

SERVES 4

butternut pumpkin 500 g, seedless part only
minute steaks 4 x 150 g, at room temperature
eggs 4
+
**melted coconut oil or good-quality
    animal fat** 80 ml (⅓ cup)
sea salt and freshly ground black pepper
south american dressing 80 ml (⅓ cup)
    (page 242)

Both of my daughters dance, and sometimes their lessons go later into the evening. I love to cook something super quick and easy when they get home, and this meal – good old steak and eggs – is one of Chilli's absolute favourites. As this dish really only takes 30 minutes from start to finish, it is something I throw together regularly for my family. The fact that it combines yummy fats and animal proteins with some delicious veg is perfect. Sometimes we dish this up for breakfast before school, too.

Preheat the oven to 220°C (200°C fan-forced). Line a baking tray with baking paper.

Cut the pumpkin into four slices about 2 cm thick, then rub the cut sides with 1 tablespoon of the coconut oil or fat and season with salt and pepper. Place the pumpkin on the prepared tray in a single layer and roast for 15 minutes, then flip and roast for a further 15 minutes, or until the pumpkin is cooked through and golden. Set aside to cool slightly.

Meanwhile, heat 2 tablespoons of the coconut oil or fat in a large frying pan over high heat. Season the steaks with salt and pepper. Cook on one side for 2 minutes, then flip and cook on the other side for 1–2 minutes (or cook to your liking). Transfer to a plate and allow to rest for 2 minutes, keeping warm.

Wipe the pan clean, place over medium heat and add the remaining 1 tablespoon of coconut oil or fat. Crack in the eggs and cook for 2 ½ minutes, or until the egg whites are set (or cook to your liking). Season with salt and pepper.

Place the pumpkin toast on serving plates and top with a minute steak and a fried egg. Spoon over the dressing and serve

BRAISED LAMB WITH CARROTS

SERVES 6

lamb shoulder 1 x 1.8 kg, bone in, scored
with a knife, at room temperature
beef bone broth 750 ml (3 cups)
(page 229)
dutch carrots 450 g (about 24), scrubbed,
trimmed and halved

+

coconut oil or good-quality animal fat
2 tablespoons
sea salt and freshly ground black pepper
greek seasoning 1 tablespoon (page 220)
mayonnaise 150 g (page 237)
coriander leaves to serve (optional)

Slowly braised is one of the most beautiful ways to eat this superb meat. Get out your slow cooker or casserole dish and give this recipe a go. I promise you will not be disappointed. I always have mayo in the fridge, as it is simple to make and goes with so many dishes. I encourage you to get good at making your own – it takes only 30 seconds to whip up with a hand-held blender or 5 minutes to whisk by hand. The braised carrots finish off this dish perfectly.

Preheat the oven to 140°C (120°C fan-forced).

Coat the lamb with the coconut oil or fat, then season with salt and pepper.

Heat a large flameproof casserole dish over medium–high heat. Add the lamb and sear on all sides until golden brown. Remove from the heat, pour in the broth and sprinkle over the Greek seasoning. Cover with the lid and transfer to the oven to braise for 3½ hours.

Remove the dish from the oven and add the carrots. Return to the oven to braise for 20 minutes, or until the meat is falling off the bone.

Carefully remove the lamb and carrots from the dish and set aside, keeping warm. Place the dish over medium heat and simmer until the lamb jus is reduced by two-thirds, about 12–15 minutes.

Thickly carve the lamb with a sharp knife. Smear some mayonnaise on six serving plates, add the carrots and lamb and serve with the lamb jus on the side. Finish with a sprinkle of coriander leaves, if desired.

BLOOD SAUSAGE LETTUCE WRAPS WITH SPICY MAYO

This could be the yummiest lettuce wrap in the history of lettuce wraps. The secret ingredient is the blood sausage – when combined with a touch of chilli mayo and some herbs you will understand why this combination works so well from your very first mouthful ... and trust me on this, it won't be your last! If you're not keen on blood sausage, then you can use paleo pork sausages and your wrap will still be super tasty.

Heat the coconut oil or fat in a large frying pan over medium heat. Add the sausages and cook until browned on all sides and just cooked through, about 8 minutes. Remove the sausages from the pan and set aside. Season with salt and pepper.

Meanwhile, combine the mayonnaise and sriracha in a bowl. Season with salt and pepper if needed.

To serve, place two cos leaves on each serving plate, top with a sausage, then scatter over the herbs and drizzle on some spicy mayo. Roll the lettuce around the sausage to form a wrap and enjoy.

SERVES 4

paleo blood sausages 4 (you may need to order these from your butcher)
mayonnaise 100 g (page 237)
sriracha chilli sauce 1 teaspoon
cos lettuce leaves 8
asian herbs (such as mint, vietnamese mint, coriander and thai basil) 1 large handful
+
coconut oil or good-quality animal fat 1 tablespoon
sea salt and freshly ground black pepper

PORK CUTLETS WITH PINEAPPLE SALSA

SERVES 2–4

pork cutlets 4 x 300 g, at room temperature
+
coconut oil or good-quality animal fat
2 tablespoons
sea salt and freshly ground black pepper
olive oil for drizzling

Pineapple Salsa

sweet pineapple ½ (about 350 g), cored and
cut into 1 cm dice
lebanese cucumbers 2, halved lengthways,
deseeded and cut into 1 cm dice
mint leaves 1 small handful, roughly chopped
long red chilli ½–1, halved, deseeded and
finely chopped (leave the seeds in if you
like it spicy)
fish sauce 3 tablespoons

I absolutely love this type of dish, where you take a pan-fried piece of meat or fish and top it with a sensational quick salsa or sauce. Pineapple with fish sauce and chilli is a heavenly marriage of flavours that goes perfectly with pork (think ham and pineapple pizza). In my opinion, there really isn't much else needed for this dish. Having said that, you could add some nuts or sesame, pumpkin or hemp seeds to the salsa for a bit of texture.

To make the salsa, place the pineapple, cucumber, mint and chilli in a bowl, add the fish sauce and mix to combine. Set aside for 20 minutes to allow the flavours to develop.

Meanwhile, heat the coconut oil or fat in a large frying pan over medium–high heat. Season the pork cutlets with salt and pepper, then add them to the pan in batches and cook for 4 minutes on each side, or until just cooked through. Transfer to a plate and allow to rest for 2 minutes, keeping warm.

Place the pork cutlets on serving plates, give the pineapple salsa a good mix and spoon over the pork. Drizzle with some olive oil and serve.

STEAK WITH TOMATO AND BASIL

SERVES 4

italian tomato sauce 400 g (page 236)
cherry tomatoes 200 g, halved
pitted kalamata olives 80 g (½ cup), halved
scotch fillet steaks 4 x 180 g
basil leaves 1 handful
+
sea salt and freshly ground black pepper
coconut oil or good-quality animal fat
   2 tablespoons
extra-virgin olive oil for drizzling

As far as flavour combinations go, tomato and basil would have to be one of the most popular ever. We have the Italians to thank for this and, in particular, their classic caprese salad of tomato, basil and mozzarella. Here, I have replaced the mozzarella with steak … as you do!

Combine the tomato sauce, cherry tomatoes and olives in a saucepan over medium heat. Bring to a simmer, then reduce the heat to medium–low and cook, stirring occasionally, for 10 minutes, or until the cherry tomatoes break down. Season with salt and pepper if needed.

Meanwhile, season the steaks generously with salt and pepper.

Heat the coconut oil or fat in a large frying pan over medium–high heat. Add the steaks and cook for 3 minutes on each side for medium–rare (or cook to your liking). Transfer to a plate and allow to rest for 5 minutes, keeping warm.

To serve, place the steaks on serving plates, spoon over the tomato and olive sauce, scatter over the basil and drizzle on the olive oil.

LIVER WITH ZUCCHINI AND BROTH

SERVES 4

lamb liver steaks 4 x 140 g, trimmed

chicken bone broth 1 litre (page 231)

zucchini 2, sliced

+

sea salt and freshly ground black pepper

coconut oil or good-quality animal fat
2 tablespoons

coriander and cumin spice blend
1 ½–2 teaspoons (page 219)

mayonnaise 100 g (page 237)

micro herbs or herb leaves of your choice
to serve

extra-virgin olive oil for drizzling

It wasn't until I became a chef that I began to properly appreciate offal for the flavour bomb it is. Then along came my passion for health and my appreciation grew and grew, as offal really stands head and shoulders above all other ingredients in terms of health benefits. This very simple preparation highlights my two favourite healthy ingredients: liver and bone broth. I hope you love this dish as much as I do.

Pat the steaks dry with paper towel and lightly season with salt and pepper.

Heat the coconut oil or fat in a large frying pan over medium–high heat. Add the steaks in two batches and cook, turning, for 5 minutes for medium (or cook to your liking). Transfer to a plate and allow to rest, lightly covered, for 5 minutes.

Meanwhile, pour the broth into a saucepan and bring to a simmer over medium heat. Stir in the spice blend, add the zucchini and simmer for 15 minutes, or until the zucchini is tender. Season with salt and pepper.

Ladle the broth and zucchini into serving bowls, then dollop on the mayonnaise. Slice the steaks and place on top. Scatter over the herbs and finish with a good grind of pepper and a drizzle of olive oil.

Tip: You can use beef, veal, chicken, pork or duck liver instead, if you like.

BRAISED SHORT RIBS AND PICKLES

If I was ever going to have a last-meal request, then I reckon this would be it ... Well, I would actually ask to have it for breakfast, to start my last day off with a bang. If you have never cooked short ribs before, I implore you to give them a go, as they are so delicious and the mouthfeel of falling-off-the-bone meat is next level. This is quite a simple recipe, with only a little spicy mayo and some pickles to round it off, as I don't want to detract from the meat itself.

SERVES 4–6

beef short ribs 2 kg, at room temperature
beef bone broth 500 ml (2 cups)
   (page 228)
dill pickles 200 g, finely sliced

+

coconut oil or good-quality animal fat
   3 tablespoons
sea salt and freshly ground black pepper
barbecue spice blend 3 tablespoons
   (page 218), plus ½ teaspoon extra for
   the mayonnaise
mayonnaise 200 g (page 237)

Preheat the oven to 120°C (100°C fan-forced).

Rub the coconut oil or fat into the short ribs and season with salt and pepper.

Heat a large flameproof casserole dish over medium–high heat. Add the beef and cook for 5 minutes on each side to brown. Set aside to cool a little.

When the beef is cool enough to handle, rub all over with the barbecue spice blend. Return to the dish, pour in the broth and cover with the lid. Transfer to the oven to braise for 8 hours, or until the beef is meltingly tender and falling off the bone.

Mix the extra ½ teaspoon of barbecue spice blend into the mayonnaise.

Gently place the ribs on a platter, ladle over some broth and serve with the pickles and spicy mayonnaise on the side.

PORK BELLY WITH CABBAGE AND APPLE

Roast pork with apple and cabbage is a beautiful flavour combination that is so very hard to resist. I remember travelling through Austria many years ago and visiting a farmhouse restaurant on the side of the road, where they cooked and sold only what they grew themselves. This is one of the dishes I enjoyed that day and I still remember how delicious it was 15 years later.

SERVES 6

boneless pork belly 1.2 kg, skin scored, at room temperature
garlic cloves 8, unpeeled
thyme sprigs 1 small handful
savoy cabbage ½ (about 600 g), cut into wedges

+

boiling water 250 ml (1 cup)
coconut oil or good-quality animal fat 2 tablespoons
sea salt and freshly ground black pepper
jus 200 ml (page 237)
apple sauce 450 g (page 228)

Preheat the oven to 240°C (220°C fan-forced) – you need to start by blasting the pork with heat.

Place the pork on a wire rack in the kitchen sink, carefully pour the boiling water over the skin, then pat dry with paper towel.

Scatter the garlic and thyme into a large, deep roasting tin.

Rub the coconut oil or fat into the pork skin, season with a good amount of salt and place on the bed of garlic and thyme. Roast for 35–40 minutes until the skin starts to bubble. Reduce the temperature to 150°C (130°C fan-forced), scatter the cabbage around the pork and pour in 500 ml (2 cups) of water (avoiding the skin). Season with salt and pepper. Continue to roast the pork for 1¼ hours, or until the flesh is very tender. Transfer to a plate and allow to rest for 15 minutes, keeping warm. If the crackling isn't crisp enough, place the pork, crackling-side up, under a hot grill for a few minutes.

Meanwhile, place the jus and apple sauce in separate saucepans and warm through, stirring occasionally.

Carve the pork into thick slices. Divide the cabbage among serving bowls, top with the pork, pour over the jus and finish with a spoonful of warm apple sauce.

SIRLOIN STEAK WITH CARAMELISED ONION AND ROCKET SALAD

SERVES 4

sirloin steaks 4 x 200 g, at room temperature
onions 2, sliced
baby rocket leaves 2 large handfuls
basil leaves (or micro basil) 1 handful
+
coconut oil or good-quality animal fat
    3 tablespoons, melted
steak seasoning 2 teaspoons (page 224)
sea salt and freshly ground black pepper
italian dressing 3 tablespoons (page 235)

Steak served with onion is very hard to beat, yet to improve upon it, I seriously suggest you make some of the spice rubs and seasonings I have included in this book (see pages 217–224). Store them in your pantry and use them to enhance meat or fish, eggs, mayo, dressings, sauces, vegetables or salads. I really see this as the best way to elevate your home cooking to another level.

Heat a barbecue grill plate to hot or a large chargrill pan over high heat.

Brush the steaks with 1 tablespoon of the coconut oil or fat and season with a good pinch of steak seasoning. Cook the steaks on one side for 4 minutes, or until golden brown, then flip and cook for a further 3 minutes for medium–rare (or cook to your liking). Transfer to a plate and rest for 4–5 minutes, keeping warm.

Reduce the heat to medium–high and add the remaining coconut oil or fat to the barbecue or pan. Add the onion and sauté for 7–8 minutes until softened and starting to caramelise. Season with salt and pepper.

Place the rocket and basil in a bowl, add the dressing and toss to lightly coat the leaves. Season the salad with a little salt and pepper to taste.

Place the steaks on serving plates, sprinkle over a little more steak seasoning, then serve with the caramelised onion and rocket salad.

INDII'S SNAGS WITH TOMATO KETCHUP

My daughter Indii is a true carnivore and loves eating all different types of meat. One of her favourite meals is the humble sausage with tomato ketchup, which is great as it's such a simple dish. I cook this meal at least once a week, and always have sausages in the fridge ready to go. I know a lot of you will wonder why this recipe is here, and it's because this book is all about keeping things simple! I get a lot of requests from home cooks wanting fewer ingredients and simpler recipes, so this one is for all of you.

Heat the coconut oil or fat in a large frying pan over medium heat. Add the sausages and cook until browned on all sides and just cooked through, about 6 minutes. Season with salt and pepper.

Place the sausages in serving bowls and serve with the salad leaves and tomato ketchup.

SERVES 2

paleo chipolata sausages 12
mixed salad leaves 2 large handfuls
+
coconut oil or good-quality animal fat
  2 tablespoons
sea salt and freshly ground black pepper
tomato ketchup 80 g (¼ cup) (page 245)

LAMB BACKSTRAPS WITH HERB AND CASHEW SALAD

SERVES 4

lamb backstraps 2 x 350 g, trimmed,
  at room temperature
**asian herbs (such as mint, vietnamese mint,
  coriander and thai basil)** 2 large handfuls,
  finely chopped
french shallots 2, finely sliced
cashews (activated if possible) 80 g
  (½ cup), toasted and chopped
+
coconut oil or good-quality animal fat
  2 tablespoons, melted
sea salt and freshly ground black pepper
thai dressing 3 tablespoons, or to taste
  (page 244)

Here is a simple formula to keep in mind when you are creating recipes: all you need is good-quality protein from the land or sea, a sauce or dressing to accompany it, some veg or salad, and, if you want to take it to the next level, add texture and spice. With this dish I have paired some beautiful lamb with a spicy dressing and a fresh herb and nut salad for texture. Job done!

Brush the lamb with the coconut oil or fat and season with salt and pepper.

Heat a large frying pan over medium–high heat. Add the lamb and cook for 3 minutes on each side for medium–rare (or cook to your liking). Transfer to a plate and allow to rest for 5 minutes, keeping warm.

Place the herbs in a bowl and mix with the shallot, cashews and thai dressing.

Slice the lamb and arrange on a platter, top with the herb and cashew salad and serve.

ROAST PORK WITH CABBAGE AND GREMOLATA

I love to add a fresh, herby sauce or dressing like this amazing gremolata to a piece of roasted meat, as I find it adds some much-needed zing. You can have a lot of fun with these types of dressings – swap out the herbs for ones you already have on hand, or add in some different spices if you wish. This is what cooking is all about. Some simple roasted cabbage helps to round out this dish.

SERVES 8

rolled pork loin 2 kg, skin scored, tied at
5 cm intervals with kitchen string,
at room temperature
savoy cabbage ½ (about 600 g), cut into
3 cm slices
plain kombucha 500 ml (2 cups)
+
sea salt and freshly ground black pepper
coconut oil or good-quality animal fat
2 tablespoons
pork seasoning 2 teaspoons (page 222)
pistachio gremolata 100 g (page 240)

Preheat the oven to 200°C (180°C fan-forced).

Season the pork generously with salt and pepper.

Heat the coconut oil or fat in a large flameproof casserole dish over medium heat, add the pork and cook, turning occasionally, for 5–10 minutes until the skin begins to brown. Turn the pork, skin-side up, in the dish. Scatter the cabbage around the pork, pour in the kombucha and bring to the boil. Remove from the heat, sprinkle over the pork seasoning, then cover with the lid and roast in the oven for 1½ hours.

Place the pork, skin-side up, in a large roasting tin and place under a hot grill for a few minutes to crisp up the crackling. Keep a close eye on the pork at all times, as the crackling can burn very quickly. Transfer to a plate and allow to rest for 5 minutes, keeping warm.

Thickly slice the pork and serve with the cabbage and some gremolata spooned over the top.

RIB-EYE ROAST

---

onions 2, sliced
beef rib-eye roast 2.2 kg, bone in,
  at room temperature
dutch carrots 16, scrubbed and trimmed
+
coconut oil or good-quality animal fat
  3 tablespoons, melted
steak seasoning 1 ½–2 tablespoons
  (page 224)
sea salt and freshly ground black pepper
jus 200 ml (page 237)

This is the type of cooking and food that really makes me happy: a perfectly roasted piece of good-quality meat teamed with a beautiful sauce and a couple of simple vegetables to complete the picture. It really doesn't have to be complicated to make delicious food. I recommend serving a little sauerkraut on the side to finish this dish off. Remove the rib-eye from the fridge 30–40 minutes before you want to cook it to allow it to come to room temperature.

Preheat the oven to 240°C (220°C fan-forced).

Line a roasting tin with baking paper and add the onion in a single layer.

Brush 2 tablespoons of the coconut oil or fat onto the beef, then rub on the steak seasoning. Place the beef on the bed of onion and roast for 15 minutes. Reduce the temperature to 180°C (160°C fan-forced) and continue to roast for 1 ¼ hours for medium–rare beef. If you prefer your beef to be medium, add an extra 10 minutes. Transfer to a plate and allow to rest, covered, for 25–30 minutes, keeping warm.

While the meat is resting, place the dutch carrots in a roasting tin and drizzle over the remaining oil or fat. Season with salt and pepper and roast for 30 minutes.

Meanwhile, pour the jus into a saucepan and bring to a simmer over medium heat.

Serve the rib-eye and onion with the carrots and the warm jus on the side.

FILLET STEAK WITH MUSHROOMS, ROCKET AND HORSERADISH

SERVES 4

eye fillet steaks 4 x 200 g, at room
  temperature
swiss brown mushrooms 300 g, halved
baby rocket leaves 2 large handfuls

+

coconut oil or good-quality animal fat
  3 tablespoons, melted
sea salt and freshly ground black pepper
chicken seasoning (page 218), to taste
horseradish sauce 125 g (page 235)
lemon wedges to serve (optional)

There are few things that go better together than horseradish and steak. To make the combination even more delicious, I love to mix the horseradish with mayo and serve up some lovely mushrooms for good measure. The result is one of the best steak meals of all time. The same flavours work well with a piece of fish, too, if you want to change things up.

Heat a barbecue hotplate to hot or a large frying pan over high heat.

Brush the steaks with 1 tablespoon of the coconut oil or fat and season with salt and pepper. Cook the steaks on one side for 4 minutes, or until golden brown, then flip and cook for a further 3 minutes for medium–rare (or cook to your liking). Transfer to a plate and allow to rest for 4–5 minutes, keeping warm.

Reduce the heat to medium–high and add the remaining coconut oil or fat to the barbecue or pan. Add the mushroom and sauté for 6–7 minutes until cooked through. Sprinkle over the chicken seasoning.

Divide the steaks among serving plates and add the mushroom and rocket. Drizzle the horseradish sauce over the steaks and serve with lemon wedges to squeeze over the rocket, if desired.

PORK BELLY WITH CAULIFLOWER MASH

SERVES 6

boneless pork belly 1.2 kg, skin scored, at room temperature
thyme leaves 1 tablespoon, to serve
dijon mustard to serve
+
boiling water 250 ml (1 cup)
coconut oil or good-quality animal fat 2 tablespoons
sea salt
jus 200 ml (page 237)
cauliflower mash 1 kg (page 230)

Pork belly is one of my favourite cuts of meat. I like to buy it in a whole slab so I have enough for a few different meals. I usually cut it into large portions and freeze some to use later. All you need to do with pork belly is to roast or braise it, or pop it into a curry or soup. This is great served with a simple cauliflower mash and a little mustard.

Preheat the oven to 240°C (220°C fan-forced) – you need to start by blasting the pork with heat.

Place the pork on a wire rack in the kitchen sink, carefully pour the boiling water over the skin, then pat dry with paper towel.

Rub the coconut oil or fat into the pork skin, season with a good amount of salt and place the pork in a large, deep roasting tin. Roast for 35–40 minutes until the skin starts to bubble. Reduce the temperature to 150°C (130°C fan-forced) and continue to roast the pork for 1 ¼ hours, or until the flesh is very tender. Transfer to a plate and allow to rest for 15 minutes, keeping warm. If the crackling isn't crisp enough, place the pork, crackling-side up, under a hot grill for a few minutes.

Meanwhile, pour the jus into a saucepan and bring to a simmer over medium heat.

Carve the pork into thick slices. Divide the cauliflower mash among serving bowls, top with the pork, then pour over the warm jus. Scatter on the thyme and serve with a dollop of mustard on the side.

ROAST LAMB WITH SHALLOTS AND PEAS

A Sunday roast is a bit of a tradition in Australia and New Zealand, and I love throwing together a yummy lamb leg for the family to enjoy. This recipe is super traditional, like the Sunday roast itself. Perhaps the best part is that any leftovers can be made into the most delicious lamb sangas or turned into a salad.

Preheat the oven to 200°C (180°C fan-forced). Line a large roasting tin with baking paper.

Add the lamb to the prepared tin, rub all over with the oil or fat, season with salt and pepper and sprinkle over the rosemary. Roast for 1 ½ hours, basting the meat occasionally with the juices in the tin. If you prefer your lamb to be well done, cook for a further 15 minutes. Halfway through cooking, scatter in the shallots and add 125 ml (½ cup) of water. Transfer the lamb to a carving board, cover loosely with foil and allow to rest for 15 minutes.

Bring a saucepan of salted water to the boil. Add the peas and cook for 5–6 minutes until tender. Drain and place in a serving bowl. Season with salt and pepper if needed.

Carve the lamb and serve with the shallots, peas and mint sauce.

SERVES 8

leg of lamb 1 x 2.5 kg, at room temperature
rosemary 2 sprigs, leaves picked
   and chopped
french shallots 10, peeled and halved
fresh or frozen peas 300 g
+
coconut oil or good-quality animal fat
   2 tablespoons
sea salt and freshly ground black pepper
mint sauce 250 ml (1 cup) (page 238)

STEAK WITH MUSHROOMS AND EGG

SERVES 2

scotch or **sirloin steaks** 2 x 200 g,
   at room temperature
portobello mushrooms 4 large, sliced
eggs 2
+
coconut oil or **good-quality animal fat**
   3 tablespoons, melted
sea salt and **freshly ground black pepper**
chicken seasoning 2 teaspoons (page 218)

Yum, yum and more yum! That's how I describe this dish. It's the perfect breakfast for any day of the week and, depending on the thickness of your steak, can be on the table in about 10 minutes. This is the way farmers would eat before working all day, and this is how I love to break my own fast.

Heat a barbecue grill plate to hot or a chargrill pan over high heat.

Brush the steaks with 1 tablespoon of the coconut oil or fat and season with a generous amount of salt and pepper. Cook for 3–3 ½ minutes on each side for medium–rare (or cook to your liking). Transfer to a plate and allow to rest for 4 minutes, keeping warm.

Meanwhile, heat 1 ½ tablespoons of the coconut oil or fat in a frying pan over medium–high heat, add the mushroom and sauté until tender, 2–4 minutes. Add 1 teaspoon of the chicken seasoning and cook for 30 seconds, or until fragrant. Set aside in a bowl and cover to keep warm.

Wipe the pan clean, place over medium heat and add the remaining coconut oil or fat. Crack in the eggs and cook for 2 ½ minutes, or until the egg whites are set (or cook to your liking). Season with salt and pepper.

Place the steaks on serving plates, top with a fried egg, add the mushroom and sprinkle over the remaining seasoning.

VEGGIES

ROASTED HONEY AND CUMIN PUMPKIN

SERVES 4–6 AS A SIDE

kent pumpkin 1 kg (about ¼), unpeeled and
　　cut into 3 cm thick wedges or pieces
honey 3 tablespoons
cumin seeds 1 tablespoon
+
coconut oil or good-quality animal fat
　　3 tablespoons, melted
sea salt and freshly ground black pepper

I think roasted pumpkin is the bee's knees. You don't have to do too much to make it shine. Pumpkin is usually on our dinner table a couple of nights a week as it goes so well with seafood and meat. For this dish, I have gone the full Monty and added honey and spice to take it to the next level of moreish deliciousness.

Preheat the oven to 200°C (180°C fan-forced). Line a baking tray with baking paper.

Place the pumpkin on the prepared tray. Drizzle on the coconut oil or fat and honey, then sprinkle over the cumin seeds, season with salt and pepper and toss to coat. Arrange the pumpkin in a single layer and roast, flipping and basting the pumpkin from time to time with the juices that have collected on the tray, for 50–55 minutes until tender and caramelised.

GREEN PAPAYA, GREEN BEAN AND TOMATO SALAD

Green papaya often features in the recipes I create at home and for good reason – I absolutely adore the texture, flavour and health benefits it brings. It is great for helping the body to digest proteins and fats, so I like to serve it alongside barbecued meat or seafood. This salad is also delicious with rare beef, pork belly, chicken or prawns added. For an absolute treat, mud crab or lobster work too. So versatile!

Place the papaya, green beans and tomato in a bowl, add the Thai dressing and toss to combine. Set aside for 30 minutes to allow the flavours to develop.

Serve the salad in a serving bowl with some Thai basil (if using) scattered over the top.

SERVES 4 AS A SIDE

green papaya 1, deseeded and cut into matchsticks
green beans 300 g, trimmed and cut into 5 cm lengths
cherry tomatoes 200 g, quartered
+
thai dressing 140 ml (page 244)
thai basil leaves to serve (optional)

CHARRED SPRING ONIONS WITH AVOCADO PUREE

SERVES 4 AS A SIDE

spring onions 2 bunches (about 20), trimmed
avocado puree 350 g (page 228)
+
coconut oil or good-quality animal fat 2 tablespoons, melted
extra-virgin olive oil for drizzling
freshly ground black pepper

There are two components to this recipe, and each is equally important. You can use them together, as I have done here, or separately as a starting point to build different dishes. The avocado puree is super easy to make and can be used in so many ways – try it as a base for a barbecued fish fillet or as a dressing for a chicken salad. On the side we have some chargrilled greens – in this case I have used spring onions, but you can easily replace these with any green veg.

Heat a barbecue hotplate to hot or a large frying pan over high heat, then brush the surface with the coconut oil or fat. Add the spring onions and cook for 30 seconds on each side, or until soft and charred.

Arrange the spring onions on a serving platter and spoon the avocado puree alongside. Drizzle over the olive oil, sprinkle with some pepper and serve.

CHARRED EGGPLANT AND TOMATO SALAD

SERVES 4–6 AS A SIDE

eggplants 2, cut into 1 cm rounds
heirloom cherry tomatoes on the vine
　200 g, snipped into 4 or 6 bunches
ground cumin 1 teaspoon
+
sea salt and freshly ground black pepper
melted coconut oil or olive oil 80 ml (⅓ cup)
greek dressing 3 tablespoons (page 233)

The simple combination of eggplant, tomato and cumin can never be underestimated when it comes to packing in a lot of flavour. The wonderful thing about a dish like this is that it can be eaten as a side to virtually anything. Try it with a delicious piece of grilled fish, alongside a roast leg of lamb or with a barbecued steak drizzled with lots of extra-virgin olive oil.

Preheat the oven to 180°C (160°C fan-forced).

Place the eggplant in a colander, sprinkle with 2 teaspoons of salt and gently toss to coat. Set aside for 15 minutes to allow the bitter juices to drain. Lightly rinse the eggplant under cold water, then pat dry with paper towel.

Place the cherry tomato bunches on a baking tray, drizzle over a little of the oil and sprinkle on some salt and pepper. Bake for 15 minutes, or until the tomatoes are softened and the skins start to blister.

Meanwhile, heat a barbecue grill plate to medium–hot or a chargrill pan over medium–high heat.

Brush the remaining oil over the eggplant, sprinkle on the cumin and some salt and pepper, then cook, turning occasionally, for 5–6 minutes until charred and tender. Transfer the eggplant to a serving plate. Arrange the roasted cherry tomatoes on top, drizzle over the Greek dressing and serve.

CAULIFLOWER SOUP

SERVES 4

cauliflower 1 head (about 1 kg), broken
  into florets
onion 1, chopped
garlic cloves 4, chopped
chicken bone broth 1.25 litres (page 231)
+
coconut oil or good-quality animal fat
  3 tablespoons, melted
sea salt and freshly ground black pepper
extra-virgin olive oil for drizzling

When cauliflower is abundant and cheap, I love to eat it in as many ways as possible. I roast, fry, pickle and use it raw in salads. One of the easiest and most satisfying ways to prepare cauliflower when you have a glut is to make a delicious soup. This one is really versatile, so use whatever seasonings take your fancy.

Preheat the oven to 200°C (180°C fan-forced).

Place one-quarter of the cauliflower florets on a baking tray, drizzle over 1 tablespoon of the coconut oil or fat and toss to coat. Sprinkle on a little salt and roast for 20 minutes, or until the cauliflower is golden. Set aside.

Heat the remaining coconut oil or fat in a large saucepan over medium–high heat. Add the onion and cook, stirring occasionally, for 5 minutes, or until slightly softened. Stir in the garlic and cook for 1 minute, or until fragrant. Add the remaining cauliflower florets and cook for 5 minutes to soften. Next, pour in the broth and bring to the boil. Reduce the heat to medium–low and simmer for 30 minutes, or until the cauliflower is very tender. Puree the soup with a hand-held blender until super smooth. Season with salt and pepper.

Ladle the soup into warm serving bowls and top with the reserved roasted cauliflower. Finish with a drizzle of olive oil, sprinkle on some pepper, if desired, and serve.

MIDDLE EASTERN KALE, CARROT AND CURRANT SALAD

Salads needn't be complicated; in fact, often the best ones are the simplest. The most important thing is to use the freshest ingredients and pair them with a delicious dressing. Here, I have teamed kale with carrot and, to add a little sweetness, some currants. Then, to balance this out, I've included an easy dressing with some much-needed healthy fats and vinegar for acidity.

Place the kale in a large bowl and pour over the olive oil. Massage the oil into the kale with your hands. (This removes the waxy coating on the kale and allows it to absorb the dressing.)

Pour the dressing over the kale, toss and leave to stand for at least 30 minutes.

Just before serving, add the carrot, sprinkle over the currants and season with salt and pepper, if needed.

SERVES 4 AS A SIDE

curly kale 1 bunch (about 300 g), stems discarded and leaves torn
carrots 2, cut into matchsticks
currants 75 g (½ cup)
+
extra-virgin olive oil 1 tablespoon
middle eastern dressing 125 ml (½ cup) (page 238)
sea salt and freshly ground black pepper if needed

INDIAN-SPICED ROASTED OKRA

SERVES 4 AS A SIDE

okra 600 g, cut in half lengthways
fresh curry leaves 40
+
melted coconut oil or good-quality
    animal fat 100 ml
indian spice blend 1 tablespoon (page 221)
sea salt and freshly ground black pepper
raita 280 g (page 241)

I'm on a mission to get more people to eat the amazing and often overlooked vegetable called okra. This wonderful ingredient works well in salads, soups, stir-fries, curries, pies and roasts, and it can be eaten raw, deep-fried, pickled or fermented. Here, I have created a spiced dish with a powerful flavour that is the perfect accompaniment to a piece of well-sourced meat or fish.

Preheat the oven to 220°C (200°C fan-forced).

Combine 3 tablespoons of the coconut oil or fat, the Indian spice blend and okra in a bowl and toss until the okra is evenly coated. Season with a little salt and pepper, then place the okra on a baking tray and spread out evenly in a single layer. Roast for 15 minutes, or until the okra is cooked through and golden.

Meanwhile, heat the remaining 2 tablespoons of coconut oil or fat in a frying pan over medium heat. Add the curry leaves and cook for 20–30 seconds, or until they are translucent and crispy. Drain on paper towel. Season with a little salt.

Arrange the roasted okra in a serving dish and scatter over the curry leaves. Spoon the raita into a small serving bowl, drizzle over a little of the oil remaining on the baking tray and serve on the side.

SWEET POTATO FRIES

Sweet potato fries have become very trendy over the last few years as people look for new and exciting ways to reinvent their favourite foods. In this case, the popular potato chip has taken on a healthier form. You can deep-fry, shallow-fry or oven-bake these fries. I am a huge fan of adding spices or herbs and serving mayo or aioli with my fries, so have a play and mix things up every time you make yours.

Dust the sweet potato with the tapioca flour.

Heat the coconut oil or fat in a large saucepan to 160°C. (To test the temperature, add a small piece of sweet potato. If tiny bubbles of oil appear at the edges, it's ready.) Working in three batches, add the sweet potato to the oil and cook for 3 minutes. Drain in a single layer on paper towel, then transfer to the fridge to chill for 1 hour, or the freezer for 15 minutes.

Separate the sweet potato fries after chilling and before deep-frying for the second time. Reheat the oil in the pan to 180°C. (To check, place a piece of sweet potato in the oil and if it immediately bubbles quite vigorously, it's ready.) Deep-fry the sweet potato fries in three batches for 2–2 ½ minutes until golden and crisp. Remove with a slotted spoon, drain on paper towel and season with the salt.

Spoon some mayonnaise into a small bowl and swirl in a spoonful of tomato ketchup.

Serve the fries with the mayo and ketchup dipping sauce on the side.

SERVES 2–4 AS A SIDE

sweet potatoes 700 g, cut into 1 cm thick batons
tapioca flour 40 g (⅓ cup) (see note page 66)

+

melted coconut oil or good-quality animal fat 600 ml
rosemary and cinnamon salt (page 223) **or sea salt** to taste
mayonnaise (page 237) to serve
tomato ketchup (page 245) to serve

JAPANESE CABBAGE SALAD

SERVES 2–4 AS A SIDE

chinese or green cabbage 400 g (about ¼),
   shredded
baby rocket leaves 2 large handfuls
nori sheets 2, finely sliced (see note)
+
japanese dressing 125 ml (½ cup)
   (page 236)
sea salt and freshly ground black pepper
   if needed

The Japanese have a wonderful respect for produce and know how to make food absolutely delicious with minimal ingredients. This tantalising cabbage salad features a very addictive umami-flavoured dressing and is perfect for you to whip up at home.

Place the cabbage and rocket in a bowl and mix to combine.

Pour the dressing over the cabbage and rocket and gently toss to coat. Season with some salt and pepper if needed.

Arrange the salad on a platter or in a salad bowl, sprinkle over the nori and serve.

Note: Nori is a dark green, paper-like, toasted seaweed used for most kinds of sushi and other Japanese dishes. Nori provides an abundance of essential nutrients and is rich in vitamins, minerals, amino acids, omega-3 and omega-6, and antioxidants. Nori sheets are commonly used to roll sushi, but they can also be added to salads and soups, and fish, meat and vegetable dishes. You can buy nori sheets from Asian grocers and most supermarkets.

ROASTED PUMPKIN WITH RED ONION, ROCKET AND HEMP SEEDS

SERVES 4–6 AS A SIDE

kent pumpkin 1 kg (about ¼), cut into 3 cm
   thick wedges
red onions 2, cut into 1 cm thick wedges
rocket leaves 2 handfuls
hemp seeds 1 tablespoon (see note)
+
coconut oil or good-quality animal fat
   3 tablespoons, melted
pumpkin spice blend 1 tablespoon
   (page 223)
sea salt and freshly ground black pepper

Hemp seeds are a wonderful ingredient to use in so many ways. Try them in smoothies or bircher muesli or in dairy-free pestos or stuffings. The simplest way to incorporate hemp seeds into your diet is to sprinkle them over salads, meat, seafood and vegetables, as I've done here with this yummy roast pumpkin dish.

Preheat the oven to 200°C (180°C fan-forced). Line a baking tray with baking paper.

Place the pumpkin on the prepared tray, drizzle on the coconut oil or fat, then sprinkle over the pumpkin spice blend, season with salt and pepper and toss to coat evenly. Arrange the pumpkin in a single layer on the tray and roast for 25 minutes. Flip the pumpkin, baste with the juices and scatter over the onion. Return to the oven to roast for a further 20–25 minutes until the pumpkin is tender and caramelised.

To serve, scatter the rocket over the pumpkin and sprinkle on the hemp seeds.

Note: Hemp seeds are rich in healthy fats and essential fatty acids. They are also a great protein source and contain high amounts of vitamin E, phosphorus, potassium, magnesium, sulphur, calcium, iron and zinc. Hemp seeds are a great source of arginine and gamma-linolenic acid, which have been linked to a reduced risk of heart disease.

CABBAGE AND BRUSSELS SPROUT SOUP

I'm sure you have heard of the cabbage soup diet and while I'm not encouraging people to eat only cabbage soup, this is tasty and quick and ideal for when you fancy a light meal. It is also just the thing if you have a cold or need a little nourishment to warm you up.

Heat the coconut oil or fat in a saucepan over medium heat. Add the cabbage and cook for 5 minutes, or until softened.

Add the brussels sprouts, broth and turmeric to the pan and stir well. Bring to the boil, reduce the heat to medium–low, cover with a lid and simmer gently for 30 minutes, or until the vegetables are tender. Season with salt and pepper.

Ladle the soup into warm bowls and serve.

SERVES 4

green cabbage 240 g, shredded
brussels sprouts 200 g (about 16), trimmed and halved
chicken bone broth 1.5 litres (page 231) (or use beef or pork bone broth)
grated fresh turmeric 1 teaspoon **(or ground turmeric** ½ teaspoon)
+
coconut oil or good-quality animal fat 2 tablespoons
sea salt and freshly ground black pepper

ROASTED CARROTS WITH NUTS AND SEEDS

SERVES 4 AS A SIDE

carrots 5 (about 900 g), sliced into rounds about 1 cm thick

ground cumin 1 teaspoon

mint leaves 2 handfuls

mixed nuts and seeds 3 tablespoons, chopped

pomegranate molasses 2 tablespoons (see note)

+

coconut oil or good-quality animal fat 2 tablespoons, melted

sea salt and freshly ground black pepper

I find that having nuts, seeds, spices and herbs on hand means you can take a simple yummy ingredient and turn it into a dinner-table star. The combination of cumin, mint, nuts and seeds in this dish is a flavour marriage made in heaven, which really brings the carrots to life.

Preheat the oven to 200°C (180°C fan-forced). Line a large baking tray with baking paper.

Place the carrot in a bowl, add the coconut oil or fat, sprinkle on the cumin, season with salt and pepper and toss to coat.

Arrange the carrot in a single layer on the prepared tray. Roast for 35–40 minutes until the carrot is lightly golden and tender. Allow to cool.

Place the carrot in a serving bowl, scatter over the mint, nuts and seeds, then drizzle over the pomegranate molasses. Toss well and serve.

Note: Pomegranate molasses is a thick, tangy and glossy reduction of pomegranate juice that is rich in antioxidants. Pomegranate molasses is used in Middle Eastern countries for glazing meat and chicken before roasting, and in sauces, salad dressings and marinades. You can buy it from Middle Eastern grocers and some delis.

ROASTED PUMPKIN SOUP

SERVES 4

butternut or kent pumpkin 800 g,
 cut into chunks
onion 1, chopped
garlic cloves 2, chopped
chicken bone broth 1 litre (4 cups)
 (page 231)
coconut cream 185 ml (¾ cup)

+

coconut oil or good-quality animal fat
 2 tablespoons, melted
sea salt and freshly ground black pepper

I was taught the art of French cookery about 30 years ago when I started my apprenticeship. In the first few months I learned that broths are the cornerstone of French cuisine; the building blocks of flavour in sauces, soups and braised dishes. Interestingly, at that time, in most French restaurants and households a soup was the first course of a meal. I do love a good broth or soup, especially in the cooler months. One of my all-time favourites, this humble pumpkin soup is made with a foundation of healthy and flavoursome broth, with some coconut cream added for a hit of healthy fats.

Preheat the oven to 200°C (180°C fan-forced).

Place the pumpkin on a baking tray, drizzle over 1 tablespoon of the coconut oil or fat and toss to coat. Roast the pumpkin for 40–45 minutes until soft and starting to caramelise at the edges.

Heat the remaining coconut oil or fat in a large saucepan over medium heat. Add the onion and cook, stirring occasionally, for 5 minutes, or until softened. Stir in the garlic and cook for 1 minute, or until fragrant. Stir in the chicken broth and bring to the boil. Reduce the heat to medium–low, add the roasted pumpkin and 100 ml of coconut cream and gently simmer for 20 minutes.

Using a hand-held blender, puree the soup until super smooth. Season with salt and pepper.

To serve, ladle the soup into serving bowls, then swirl in the remaining coconut cream. Finish with a good grind of pepper.

ROASTED CAULIFLOWER WITH TAHINI AND SUMAC

SERVES 4 AS A SIDE

cauliflower 1 head (about 1 kg), broken into small florets
mint leaves 1 large handful
sumac large pinch, or to taste (see note)

+

coconut oil or good-quality animal fat 2 tablespoons, melted
sea salt and freshly ground black pepper
tahini dressing 75 g (page 243)

Middle Eastern flavours appear in my home cooking more and more these days. I think this started when I first introduced tahini and sumac to my pantry. The combination of these two ingredients can elevate the humblest of ingredients, such as roasted cauliflower, to another realm, making them the star of the dinner table. This dish works beautifully alongside lamb cutlets, pan-fried crispy skin salmon or trout, or even a roast chook.

Preheat the oven to 200°C (180°C fan-forced).

Drizzle the coconut oil or fat over the cauliflower and toss to coat.

Scatter the cauliflower in a single layer on a baking tray and season with salt and pepper. Roast for 30 minutes until the cauliflower is golden.

Drizzle half the tahini dressing on a platter, arrange the cauliflower on top, scatter over the mint, drizzle on the remaining tahini dressing and finish with a sprinkle of sumac.

Note: Sumac is a spice made from red sumac berries that have been dried and crushed. It has antimicrobial properties and a tangy, lemony flavour, which makes it ideal for pairing with seafood. It's also delicious in salad dressings. You can buy it from Middle Eastern grocers, delicatessens and some supermarkets.

MUSHROOM AND GARLIC BROTH

SERVES 4

field, portobello or cup mushrooms
500 g, sliced
garlic cloves 6, chopped
chicken bone broth 1.5 litres, plus extra
if needed (page 231)
+
coconut oil or good-quality animal fat
2 tablespoons
sea salt and freshly ground white pepper
micro herbs to serve (optional)

Mushrooms are gaining a reputation as a powerful superfood. There are many different varieties, each with different health properties, so do some research and investigate the wide range of amazing medicinal mushrooms on offer. In the meantime, you can make this delicious soup using an assortment of mushrooms, such as button, Swiss brown, shiitake, enoki, king George, chanterelles, morels, lion's mane, chestnut ... the list goes on and on and on.

Heat the coconut oil or fat in a large saucepan over medium heat. Add the mushroom and sauté until soft and tender, 6–7 minutes. Add the garlic and sauté for 1 minute, or until fragrant. Stir in the chicken broth and bring to the boil. Reduce the heat to medium–low and simmer for 30 minutes.

Puree the soup with a hand-held blender until smooth. Add more hot broth if the soup is too thick. Season with salt and white pepper, scatter over the micro herbs (if using) and serve.

SPICE MIXES

BARBECUE SPICE BLEND

MAKES 140 G

sea salt flakes 60 g
smoked paprika 3 tablespoons
onion powder 2 tablespoons
garlic powder 1 tablespoon

Place all the ingredients in a bowl and mix to combine. Store in an airtight container in the pantry for up to 3 months.

CHICKEN SEASONING

MAKES 110 G

sea salt flakes 65 g (½ cup)
finely chopped thyme leaves 2 tablespoons
finely grated lemon zest 2 tablespoons
garlic granules 2 tablespoons

Preheat the oven to 60°C or the lowest possible setting. Line a baking tray with baking paper.

Place all the ingredients in a bowl and mix to combine. Tip the mixture onto the prepared tray and spread out to form an even layer. Toast in the oven for 1 hour, or until completely dry. Allow to cool. Store in an airtight container in the pantry for up to 3 months.

CORIANDER AND CUMIN SPICE BLEND

MAKES 50 G

coriander seeds 2 tablespoons
cumin seeds 2 tablespoons
smoked paprika 1 ½ teaspoons
freshly ground black pepper 1 teaspoon
salt flakes 20 g

Place the coriander and cumin seeds in a spice grinder, or use a mortar and pestle, and grind until fine. Add the smoked paprika, salt and pepper and mix well. Store in an airtight container in the pantry for up to 3 months.

FISH SEASONING

MAKES 110 G

sea salt flakes 80 g
finely chopped flat-leaf parsley leaves 2 tablespoons
   (**or dried parsley** 2 teaspoons)
finely grated lemon zest 1 ½ tablespoons
garlic granules 1 tablespoon

Preheat the oven to 60°C or the lowest possible setting. Line a baking tray with baking paper.

Place all the ingredients in a bowl and mix to combine. Tip the mixture onto the prepared tray and spread out to form an even layer. Toast in the oven for 1 hour, or until completely dry. Allow to cool. Store in an airtight container in the pantry for up to 3 months.

GREEK SEASONING

MAKES ABOUT 110 G

sea salt flakes 80 g (¾ cup)
dried oregano 2 tablespoons
finely grated lemon zest 1 tablespoon
garlic powder 3 teaspoons

Preheat the oven to 60°C or the lowest possible setting. Line a baking tray with baking paper.

Place all the ingredients in a bowl and mix to combine. Tip the mixture onto the prepared tray and spread out to form an even layer. Toast in the oven for 1 hour, or until completely dry. Allow to cool. Store in an airtight container in the pantry for up to 3 months.

HEALING SPICE BLEND

MAKES 90 G

sea salt flakes 65 g (½ cup)
ground turmeric 1 tablespoon
ground ginger 2 teaspoons
garlic powder 2 teaspoons

Place all the ingredients in a bowl and mix to combine. Store in an airtight container in the pantry for up to 3 months.

INDIAN SPICE BLEND

MAKES 120 G

sea salt flakes 80 g (¾ cup)
curry powder 3 tablespoons
ground ginger 1 teaspoon
garlic powder 1 teaspoon

Place all the ingredients in a bowl and mix to combine. Store in an airtight container in the pantry for up to 3 months.

JAPANESE SPICE BLEND

MAKES 50 G

finely grated orange zest 2 tablespoons
chilli flakes 3 tablespoons
sesame seeds 2 tablespoons
salt flakes 30 g

Preheat the oven to 60°C or the lowest possible setting. Line a baking tray with baking paper.

Spread the orange zest on the prepared tray in a single layer. Bake for 2 hours, or until completely dry. Cool.

Finely grind the chilli flakes in a spice grinder or using a mortar and pestle. Transfer to a bowl and mix in the orange zest, sesame seeds and salt. Store in an airtight container in the pantry for up to 3 months.

MIDDLE EASTERN SPICE BLEND

MAKES 140 G

sea salt flakes 100 g
sumac 2 tablespoons (see note page 212)
ground cumin 2 tablespoons
dried oregano 1 tablespoon

Place all the ingredients in a bowl and mix to combine. Store in an airtight container in the pantry for up to 3 months.

PORK SEASONING

MAKES 120 G

sea salt flakes 80 g (¾ cup)
finely chopped sage leaves 2 tablespoons
crushed fennel seeds 2 ½ tablespoons
ground cumin 1 ½ tablespoons

Preheat the oven to 60°C or the lowest possible setting. Line a baking tray with baking paper.

Place all the ingredients in a bowl and mix to combine. Spread the mixture on the prepared tray in an even layer and bake for 1 hour, or until completely dry. Allow to cool. Store in an airtight container in the pantry for up to 3 months.

PUMPKIN SPICE BLEND

MAKES 50 G

ground cumin 3 tablespoons
ground cinnamon 1 tablespoon
finely chopped rosemary leaves 1 tablespoon
salt flakes 30 g

Place all the ingredients in a bowl and mix to combine. Store in an airtight container in the pantry for up to 3 months.

ROSEMARY AND CINNAMON SALT

MAKES 95 G

ground cinnamon 2 teaspoons
finely chopped rosemary leaves 1 tablespoon
sea salt flakes 80 g (¾ cup)

Place all the ingredients in a bowl and mix to combine. Store in an airtight container in the pantry for up to 3 months.

STEAK SEASONING

MAKES 90 G

chilli flakes 3 teaspoons
finely chopped rosemary leaves 1 ½ tablespoons
   (**or dried rosemary** 1 ½ teaspoons)
finely grated lemon zest 2 teaspoons
sea salt flakes 80 g (¾ cup)

Place all the ingredients in a bowl and mix to combine.
Store in an airtight container in the pantry for up to
3 months.

TURMERIC SPICE RUB

MAKES 230 G

garlic cloves 10, chopped
finely grated fresh turmeric 1 tablespoon
lemongrass stems 2, pale part only, finely chopped
lemon juice 1 tablespoon
fish sauce 1 tablespoon

Place all the ingredients in a high-speed blender or
food processor, add 80 ml (⅓ cup) of water and blend
to form a fine paste. Store in an airtight container in the
fridge for up to 1 week.

SAUCES, DRESSINGS & SIDES

APPLE SAUCE

MAKES 450 G

coconut oil 1 ½ tablespoons
granny smith apples 3, peeled, cored and sliced
honey 1 ½ tablespoons (optional)
ground cinnamon ¼ teaspoon
sea salt and freshly ground black pepper to taste

Melt the coconut oil in a frying pan over medium–low heat. Add the apple and 3 tablespoons of water, cover with a lid and cook for 10 minutes. Stir in the honey (if using) and cinnamon, cover with a lid and cook, stirring occasionally, for 5 minutes, or until the apple is soft.

Puree the apple mixture in a blender or food processor and season to taste. Set aside to cool. Store in an airtight container in the fridge for up to 2 weeks.

AVOCADO PUREE

MAKES 350 G

avocados 2, diced
garlic clove 1, finely grated
lemon juice 2 tablespoons, or to taste
sea salt and freshly ground black pepper
extra-virgin olive oil for drizzling

Place the avocado, garlic and lemon juice in a food processor and blend until smooth. Season with salt and pepper and serve with a good drizzle of olive oil. Store in an airtight container in the fridge for up to 4 days.

BEEF BONE BROTH

MAKES 3.5–4 LITRES

**meaty beef rib or neck bones, beef knuckles
and marrow bones** 4 kg
onions 3, roughly chopped
celery stalks 3, roughly chopped
thyme sprigs 8
black peppercorns 1 teaspoon, crushed
garlic bulb 1, cut in half horizontally

Preheat the oven to 200°C (180°C fan-forced).

Divide the bones between a few large roasting tins and
roast for 30–40 minutes until well browned.

Transfer the bones to a stockpot and add the vegetables.

Pour the fat from the roasting tins into a saucepan,
add 1 litre of water, place over high heat and bring to
a simmer, stirring with a wooden spoon to loosen any
coagulated juices.

Add this liquid to the bones and vegetables, then pour
in 4 litres of water to just cover the bones. The liquid
should come no higher than 2 cm from the rim of the
pot, as the volume will expand slightly during cooking.

Bring the broth to the boil, skimming off the scum
that rises to the top. Reduce the heat to low and add
the thyme, peppercorns and garlic. Cover the pot and
simmer for 12–24 hours. The longer you cook the
broth the richer and more flavourful it will be.

Strain the broth into a large container, cover and place
in the fridge overnight. Remove the congealed fat that
rises to the top and reserve for cooking (it will keep in
the fridge for up to 1 week or in the freezer for up to
3 months).

Transfer the thick and gelatinous broth to smaller
airtight containers and place in the fridge or, for long-
term storage, the freezer. The broth will keep for up to
4 days in the fridge or up to 3 months in the freezer.

CAESAR DRESSING

MAKES 230 G

salted anchovy fillets 8, rinsed and patted dry, finely chopped
garlic cloves 1–2, finely grated
mayonnaise 200 g (page 237)
sea salt and freshly ground black pepper to taste

Place all the ingredients in a bowl, add 1 tablespoon of water and mix to combine. Taste and season with a little more salt and pepper if needed. Store in an airtight glass jar in the fridge for up to 1 week.

CAULIFLOWER MASH

MAKES 1 KG

cauliflower 1 large head (about 1.3 kg), chopped into florets
coconut oil or good-quality animal fat 2 tablespoons, melted
sea salt and freshly ground black pepper
almonds, thyme leaves and olive oil to serve (optional)

Fill a saucepan with water and place a steamer basket with a lid on top. Bring to the boil, place the cauliflower florets in the steamer, cover and steam for 30–35 minutes until the cauliflower is very soft. Place the cauliflower in a food processor and whiz until smooth. Add the coconut oil or fat and whiz again. Season with salt and pepper and serve with optional garnishes, if desired.

CHICKEN BONE BROTH

MAKES 4.5 LITRES

bony chicken parts 3 kg (necks, backs, breastbones, wings)
onion 1 large, roughly chopped
carrots 2, roughly chopped
celery stalks 3, roughly chopped
garlic bulb 1, cut in half horizontally

Place the chicken pieces in a stockpot, then add 5 litres of cold water and the remaining ingredients. Place the pot over medium–high heat and bring to the boil, skimming off the scum that forms on the surface of the liquid. Reduce the heat to low and simmer for 6–12 hours.

Strain the broth through a fine sieve into a large storage container, then cover and place in the fridge overnight until the fat rises to the top and congeals. Skim off the fat and reserve for cooking; it will keep in the fridge for up to 1 week or in the freezer for up to 3 months. Transfer the broth to smaller airtight containers and store in the fridge for 3–4 days or freeze for up to 3 months.

CHINESE BROTH

MAKES 700 ML

chicken bone broth 700 ml (see above)
   (or fish bone broth)
tamari 1 ½ tablespoons
sesame oil 1 ½ teaspoons
sea salt and freshly ground black pepper if needed

Pour the broth into a saucepan and stir in the tamari and sesame oil. Place over medium heat and bring to a simmer to heat through. Taste, and add a little salt and pepper if needed. Store in an airtight container in the fridge for up to 2 weeks or in the freezer for up to 3 months.

CHINESE DRESSING

MAKES 275 ML

tamari 2 tablespoons
chicken bone broth 250 ml (1 cup) (page 231)
sesame oil 1 tablespoon
sea salt and freshly ground black pepper (optional)

Place the tamari, chicken bone broth and sesame oil in a bowl, whisk to combine and season with salt and pepper, if desired. Store in an airtight glass jar in the fridge for up to 1 week.

COCKTAIL SAUCE

MAKES 300 G

worcestershire sauce 1 tablespoon
mayonnaise 250 g (1 cup) (page 237)
tomato ketchup 90 g (⅓ cup) (page 245)
sea salt and freshly ground black pepper to taste

Combine all the ingredients in a bowl and mix well. Taste and season with more salt and pepper if needed. Store in an airtight container in the fridge for up to 1 week.

FRENCH DRESSING

MAKES ABOUT 200 ML

extra-virgin olive oil 125 ml (½ cup)
lemon juice 80 ml (⅓ cup) (about 2 lemons)
finely chopped chervil 1 tablespoon
sea salt and freshly ground black pepper

Place the olive oil, lemon juice and chervil in a large bowl and whisk to combine. Season with salt and pepper. Store in an airtight glass jar in the fridge for up to 1 week.

GREEK DRESSING

MAKES ABOUT 200 ML

lemon juice 80 ml (⅓ cup) (about 2 lemons)
extra-virgin olive oil 125 ml (½ cup)
dried oregano 2 tablespoons
sea salt and freshly ground black pepper

Combine the lemon juice, olive oil and oregano in a large bowl and whisk well. Season with salt and pepper. Store in an airtight glass jar in the fridge for up to 1 week.

HERB SAUCE

MAKES ABOUT 250 ML

tarragon leaves 3 tablespoons
flat-leaf parsley leaves 3 tablespoons
dill fronds 3 tablespoons
extra-virgin olive oil 200 ml
sea salt and freshly ground black pepper to taste

Place all the ingredients in a food processor and blend to a chunky sauce. Store in an airtight glass jar in the fridge for up to 1 week.

HOISIN SAUCE

MAKES ABOUT 220 ML

tamari 125 ml (½ cup)
raw honey 80 g
tahini 2 tablespoons
chinese five spice ¼ teaspoon
sea salt and freshly ground black pepper to taste

Place all the ingredients in a bowl and mix until smooth. Store in an airtight glass jar in the fridge for up to 3 weeks.

HORSERADISH SAUCE

MAKES ABOUT 280 G

finely grated fresh horseradish 1 tablespoon
lemon juice 1–2 teaspoons, or to taste
mayonnaise 250 g (1 cup) (page 237)
sea salt and freshly ground black pepper

Place all the ingredients in a bowl and mix to combine. Store in an airtight glass jar in the fridge for up to 5 days.

ITALIAN DRESSING

MAKES ABOUT 300 ML

balsamic vinegar 80 ml (⅓ cup)
extra-virgin olive oil 200 ml
basil leaves 10, finely chopped (you can also use micro basil leaves)
finely chopped oregano leaves 1 teaspoon
sea salt and freshly ground black pepper

Combine the balsamic vinegar, olive oil, basil and oregano in a large bowl whisk well. Season with salt and pepper. Store in an airtight glass jar in the fridge for up to 5 days.

ITALIAN TOMATO SAUCE

MAKES 700 G

coconut oil or good-quality animal fat 2 tablespoons
onion 1, chopped
garlic cloves 6, finely sliced
whole peeled tomatoes 800 g, crushed
sea salt and freshly ground black pepper

Heat the coconut oil or fat in a saucepan over medium heat, add the onion and cook for 5 minutes until softened. Stir in the garlic and cook for 1 minute until fragrant. Add the tomato and 125 ml (½ cup) of water and simmer for 25–30 minutes until thickened. Season to taste, transfer to a blender and blend until smooth. Store in an airtight glass jar in the fridge for up to 2 weeks.

JAPANESE DRESSING

MAKES 140 ML

apple cider vinegar 3 tablespoons
tamari 3 tablespoons
extra-virgin olive oil 80 ml (⅓ cup)
sea salt and freshly ground black pepper (optional)

Place the vinegar and tamari in a bowl and whisk to combine, then slowly add the olive oil and whisk until emulsified. Season with salt and pepper, if desired, then store in an airtight glass jar in the fridge for up to 1 month.

JUS

MAKES 400 ML

tomato paste 1 tablespoon
coconut oil or good-quality animal fat 1 tablespoon
red wine 250 ml (1 cup)
beef bone broth 1.5 litres (page 229)
sea salt and freshly ground black pepper

Add the tomato paste and coconut oil or fat to a saucepan over medium heat and cook, stirring constantly, for 1 minute. Stir in the wine, bring to the boil and simmer until reduced by two-thirds. Add the broth and bring to the boil. Turn the heat down to low and simmer, occasionally skimming the scum from the surface, until the jus is reduced by two-thirds to a sauce-like consistency. Strain through a sieve, season with salt and pepper and serve. Store in an airtight glass jar in the fridge for up to 2 weeks or freeze for up to 3 months.

MAYONNAISE

MAKES ABOUT 400 G

egg yolks 4
dijon mustard 1 ½ tablespoons
apple cider vinegar 2 tablespoons, or to taste
mild-flavoured olive oil or macadamia oil 400 ml
sea salt and freshly ground black pepper

Place the egg yolks, mustard, vinegar, oil and a pinch of salt in a glass jug and blend with a hand-held blender until smooth and creamy. Season with salt and pepper. Alternatively, place the egg yolks, mustard, vinegar and a pinch of salt in a food processor and process until combined. With the motor running, slowly pour in the oil in a thin stream and process until the mayonnaise is thick and creamy. Season with salt and pepper. Store in a sealed glass jar in the fridge for up to 5 days.

MIDDLE EASTERN DRESSING

MAKES ABOUT 240 ML

lemon juice 1 tablespoon
pomegranate molasses 80 ml (⅓ cup)
  (see note page 209)
extra-virgin olive oil 125 ml (½ cup)
sumac 1 teaspoon (see note page 212)
sea salt and freshly ground black pepper

Place the lemon juice, pomegranate molasses,
olive oil and sumac in a bowl and whisk to combine.
Season with salt and pepper. Store in an airtight glass
jar in the fridge for up to 1 week.

MINT SAUCE

MAKES ABOUT 250 ML

mint leaves 3 large handfuls, finely chopped
apple cider vinegar 80 ml (⅓ cup)
honey 1 tablespoon
olive oil 100 ml
sea salt to taste

Place all the ingredients in a bowl and whisk to
combine. Store in an airtight glass jar in the fridge
for up to 4 days.

NORI PASTE

MAKES ABOUT 350 G

dashi (or chicken bone broth) 500 ml (2 cups)
  (page 231) (or use fish bone broth)
nori sheets 10, torn into pieces (see note page 203)
tamari 1 ½ tablespoons

Pour the dashi or broth into a small saucepan and place over medium–low heat. Add the nori and tamari and bring to a simmer. Cook for 3 minutes, or until the nori has absorbed the liquid.

Transfer the nori mixture to a high-speed blender and blend until smooth. Store in an airtight container in the fridge for up to 1 week.

PESTO

MAKES 150 G

basil leaves 40 g (1 cup, firmly packed)
pine nuts 2 tablespoons
lemon juice 2 tablespoons
olive oil 125 ml (½ cup)
sea salt and freshly ground black pepper to taste

Place all the ingredients in a food processor and whiz to a thick paste. Store in an airtight container in the fridge for up to 4 days.

PICKLED RED ONION

MAKES 200 G

red onion ½, cut into 8 wedges
red wine vinegar 80 ml (⅓ cup)
fresh bay leaves 2
honey 1 tablespoon
sea salt and freshly ground black pepper

Place the onion, vinegar, bay leaves and honey in a small saucepan and bring to a simmer over medium heat. Cover with a lid and cook for 1 minute, then remove from the heat and allow to cool completely. Season with salt and pepper.

Store in an airtight glass container in the fridge for up to 2 months.

PISTACHIO GREMOLATA

MAKES 130 G

finely chopped flat-leaf parsley leaves 20 g (½ cup)
finely chopped toasted pistachio kernels
  3 tablespoons
garlic clove 1, finely chopped
lemon zest and juice of ½, or to taste.
sea salt and freshly ground black pepper
extra-virgin olive oil 3 tablespoons

Combine all the ingredients in a small bowl and set aside for 15 minutes to allow the flavours to develop. Store in an airtight container in the fridge for up to 5 days.

RAITA

MAKES 280 G

lebanese cucumber ½
coconut yoghurt 200 g
ground cumin 1 teaspoon
finely chopped mint leaves 2 tablespoons
sea salt and freshly ground black pepper
lemon juice to taste (optional)

Cut the cucumber in half lengthways and use a teaspoon to scrape out the seeds. Coarsely grate the cucumber flesh and squeeze out the excess liquid with your hands.

Combine the grated cucumber, coconut yoghurt, cumin and mint in a bowl and stir well. Season to taste and add a squeeze of lemon juice, if desired. Store in an airtight container in the fridge for up to 5 days. Mix well before serving.

ROMESCO SAUCE

MAKES 450 G

red capsicums 3
coconut oil for brushing (optional)
almonds (activated, if possible) 40 g (¼ cup), toasted
red wine vinegar 2 ½ tablespoons
extra-virgin olive oil 3 tablespoons
sea salt and freshly ground black pepper

Cook the capsicums, turning frequently, over an open flame on a stovetop or barbecue for 8–10 minutes until the skin is charred and the flesh feels soft when pressed. Alternatively, preheat the oven to 240°C (220°C fan-forced). Place the capsicums on a baking tray, brush with the coconut oil and roast for 15 minutes.

Place the charred capsicums in a large bowl, cover tightly and set aside to cool.

Transfer the cooled capsicums to a colander to drain, then peel and discard the skins, seeds and stalks. Place the capsicum flesh in a food processor, add the almonds and vinegar and whiz. Pour in the olive oil and process until smooth. Season with salt and pepper. If the sauce is too thick, mix in a little cold water. Store in an airtight container in the fridge for up to 1 week.

SAUCE VIERGE

MAKES ABOUT 380 G

extra-virgin olive oil 80 ml (⅓ cup)
lemon juice 2 tablespoons
coriander seeds 1 ½ teaspoons, toasted and crushed
tomatoes 2, peeled, deseeded and diced
sea salt and freshly ground black pepper

Gently warm the olive oil in a saucepan. Remove from the heat, mix in the lemon juice and coriander seeds and leave for 2 minutes. Add the tomato and season with salt and pepper. Store in an airtight container in the fridge for up to 1 week.

SOUTH AMERICAN DRESSING

MAKES 200 ML

chopped coriander leaves 30 g (⅓ cup) (about 1 bunch)
lime juice 125 ml (½ cup)
extra-virgin olive oil 125 ml (½ cup)
sea salt and freshly ground black pepper

Place the coriander, lime juice and olive oil in a bowl and mix to combine. Season with salt and pepper. Store in an airtight glass jar in the fridge for up to 1 week.

TAHINI DRESSING

MAKES 150 G

hulled tahini 3 tablespoons
lemon juice 2 tablespoons
garlic clove 1, finely grated
sea salt and freshly ground black pepper

Place the tahini, lemon juice and garlic in a small bowl, add 3 tablespoons of water and mix to combine. Season to taste with salt and pepper. Store in an airtight container in the fridge for up to 2 weeks.

TAMARI AND GINGER MARINADE

MAKES 230 ML

finely grated ginger 1 tablespoon
tamari 100 ml
honey 100 g
finely chopped spring onion 2 teaspoons

Place all the ingredients in a bowl and mix to combine. Store in an airtight container in the fridge for up to 1 week.

TARTARE SAUCE

MAKES 270 G

salted capers 1 tablespoon, rinsed and patted dry, finely chopped
cornichons 1 tablespoon, finely chopped
chopped dill fronds 1 tablespoon
mayonnaise 250 g (½ cup) (page 237)
sea salt and freshly ground black pepper to taste

Place all the ingredients in a bowl and mix to combine. Taste and season with more salt and pepper if needed. Store in an airtight container in the fridge for up to 1 week.

THAI DRESSING

MAKES 200 ML

fish sauce 3 tablespoons, or to taste
lime juice 90 ml, or to taste
honey 1 ½ tablespoons, or to taste
finely chopped coriander roots 1 ½ teaspoons
long red chillies 1–2, halved, deseeded and roughly chopped

Combine all the ingredients in a blender until the chilli is finely chopped. Taste and add more fish sauce, lime juice or honey if necessary. Store in an airtight container in the fridge for up to 3 weeks.

TOMATO KETCHUP

MAKES 330 G

tomato paste 180 g
apple cider vinegar 1 tablespoon
garlic powder 1 teaspoon
onion powder 1 teaspoon
ground cinnamon ½ teaspoon
honey 1 teaspoon

Mix the tomato paste with 100 ml of water in a small saucepan. Place over medium heat and bring to a simmer (add more water if you prefer your sauce to be thinner). Remove from the heat and stir in the remaining ingredients until incorporated and smooth. Cool and store in an airtight glass jar in the fridge for up to 4 weeks.

THANKS

A mountain of gratitude to my glorious family, especially my wonderful wife, Nic, and my two amazing daughters, Indii and Chilli. You three angels are a constant source of pure inspiration and happiness, and it is a humbling honour to walk beside you all throughout this life.

To the absolute wonder twins, Monica and Jacinta Cannataci, you both add your own magic essence to everything we create together, and this book just wouldn't be the same without your input. Thank you both for working so graciously and tirelessly, and for all that you do!

To the incredible photography and styling team of William Meppem, Chris Middleton, Steve Brown, Rob Palmer, Mark Roper, Lucy Tweed, Lee Blaylock and Deb Kaloper. You all bring a unique sense of beauty that never ceases to amaze, and I'm endlessly thankful to you all.

To Ingrid Ohlsson and Mary Small, thank you for passionately orchestrating the path that allows so much goodness to come to life. It is a pleasure to work with you both, always!

Thanks to Clare Marshall, for making sure everything is as it should be. It is a joy to have you crossing the T's and dotting the I's.

To Clare Keighery, thanks for being the best publicist any author could wish to work with.

To Megan Johnston, thanks for your careful and thorough editing.

To Emily O'Neill, thank you for creating such a gorgeous design.

A very warm thank you to my sweet mum, Joy. Among many things, you passed on your love of cooking and there's no doubt that I wouldn't be where I am without you.

A huge thanks to my teachers, peers, mentors and friends, who are all working towards creating a healthier world and who are all in their own right true forces for good: Nora Gedgaudas and Lisa Collins, Trevor Hendy, Rudy Eckhardt, Dr Pete Bablis, Dr David Perlmutter, Dr Alessio Fasano, Dr Kelly Brogan, Dr William Davis, Dr Joseph Mercola, Helen Padarin, Dr Natasha Campbell-McBride, Dr Frank Lipman, Dr Libby, Prof. Tim Noakes, Pete Melov and Prof. Martha Herbert, to name a few.

INDEX

A PLUM BOOK

First published in 2019 by
Pan Macmillan Australia Pty Limited
Level 25, 1 Market Street,
Sydney, NSW 2000, Australia

Level 3, 112 Wellington Parade,
East Melbourne, VIC 3002, Australia

Design by Emily O'Neill

Edited by Megan Johnston

Index by Helena Holmgren

Photography by William Meppem, with additional
photography by Steve Brown, Chris Middleton,
Rob Palmer and Mark Roper

Prop and food styling by Lee Blaylock, Deborah Kaloper
and Lucy Tweed

Food preparation by Jacinta and Monica Cannataci

Typeset by Emily O'Neill

Colour reproduction by Splitting Image Colour Studio

Printed and bound in China by 1010 Printing International
Limited

A CIP catalogue record for this book is available from
the National Library of Australia.